AFTER THE COSSACKS BURNED DOWN THE "Y"

By the same author

ME AND MY RUSSIAN WIFE | TROIKA

After the Cossacks burned down the "Y"

by Eddy Gilmore

FARRAR, STRAUS AND COMPANY | NEW YORK

★

TO MARY ELIZABETH
AND JOSEPH

Contents

AFTER THE COSSACKS BURNED
DOWN THE "Y"

1. Newspapermen
Aren't News

My first physical contact with Russia came in the early days of World War II, when I landed from an Arctic Ocean convoy in Archangel. I was then a highly unsophisticated and aging country boy of thirty-two; I was forty-four when I finally got away. Twelve years are a large part of a man's life. During those years Russia both fascinated and repelled me, and I lived and worked in a maddening affinity of American-Slavic love-hate. For me this vast country of contradictions and paradoxes was, at one time or another, sad-gay, tragic-happy, deadly dull-highly interesting, frustrating-inspiring, indifferent-tantalizing, hostile-friendly—and sometimes all these things at once.

"How'd you like to go back to Russia?" asked one of our officials during his visit to Britain.

To go back after an absence of ten years, after making a comfortable home in England and learning to live happily in its soft and incessant rain, after increasing the Gilmore family total by a third daughter—well, was it prudent? I could not make up my mind, but as I am a foreign correspondent and a member of that large news-gathering and news-distributing organization, The Associated Press, the decision was not altogether mine.

"After all these years?"

"After all these years."

"Well, it's certainly an appropriate time. The twentieth anniversary of the battle of Stalingrad comes on February 2nd, and the tenth anniversary of Stalin's death on March 5th."

"A perfect time."

In the field of competitive journalism, timing is an all-important factor. Newspapers, magazines, radio and television networks, and certainly the news agencies were constantly in search of an appropriate peg on which to hang news stories. March fifth, 1963, a decade after Stalin's death —that was a stout peg all right on which to display a comparison of Stalin's Russia with the Russia of his amazing successor, Nikita S. Khrushchev, a man who has always reminded me of a wily and highly articulate samovar salesman from Omsk turned politician.

"I'd like it immensely," I said. "It should make a hell of a story, but—"

"But what?" asked Wes Gallagher, general manager of the AP.

"Tamara," I told him.

"What about Tamara? She's no longer a Soviet citizen. She's an American."

"Yes and no," said I. "She has an American passport, but in the eyes of the Russians she's technically a Soviet citizen. To give up Soviet nationality you have to make a formal renunciation before the Supreme Soviet. She hasn't done that."

"Must she go back with you?"

"You know, someone once said that Russians make the world's worst immigrants, and no matter how long they are away from Russia, they all want to go back. Tamara certainly wants to. She hasn't seen her mother, sister or brother for ten years. They're all in Moscow. She would never understand if I didn't offer to take her back. But, and this is a big one, is it safe?"

"You should know if anyone does. You lived there long enough."

"I know. I know."

The point was—I did not know.

For one thing I am no expert on Russia. A friend of mine has evolved the theory that there is no such thing as a Russian expert. He says there are only varying degrees of ignorance, and I am inclined to agree.

If my wife went back, would she be let out again? How could I be certain?

As I travelled home by train that evening I tried to be logical. Other Russian girls married to foreigners visited their families in the U.S.S.R., and there had been no difficulties about leaving. Why should it be any different for Tamara? And at one of those Geneva Conferences had not Mr. Khrushchev himself—in a brief informal exchange—suggested that I make a return journey to Moscow and take my wife?

The more I thought about it the better I felt about it. And yet . . . Had not an esteemed official of the State Department, a man whose judgment I trust, warned me that if Tamara ever went back she should pick an appropriate time, such as the week before a big East-West conference when the Kremlin would be less ready to impose new problems for Washington? "Mind you," he emphasized, "I said the week *before* such a conference, not the week *after*." The trouble was, the East and West were not conferring in the winter of 1963. Worse, every few months seemed to bring on new spy scares and melodramatic accusations in Moscow, Washington and London. And yet . . .

At home that night, with no preliminaries or build up, I announced as casually as I dared, "The AP wants me to make a trip to Moscow."

Tamara's big brown eyes widened. For ten years her

principal dream and main topic of conversation had been visiting her relatives one day. I had seen her eyes cloud with tears on seeing photographs of familiar places in the land of her birth, or on hearing Russian songs, particularly those blue-noted Russian gypsy laments of spent summers and lost loves. Yet when I made my announcement all she could manage was a gasp and that single English word, "Really?" She did, however, manage to put a mountain of feeling into it.

"It's better than that," I told her. "You can go too. That is, if you want to."

"Me? Moscow? Go back? Oh, Hoaney (this is the way she has always pronounced Honey), when?"

"Soon. But you must be sure. I more or less have to go. For me it's a job. For you—well, this is something I want you to decide for yourself."

"Of course I want to go. Of course I will go. But the children?" Suddenly there was deep anxiety in her voice. "I don't think we'd better take them."

"How could we?" I asked. "They are in school."

"Yes, of course."

She seemed relieved at having this decision made for her, and then she became excited all over again.

"You mean we're really going back to Moscow?"

"If the Soviet authorities will let us."

"You mean they might not?"

"I'm not sure. You know I don't have much visa appeal."

Within a few days my company decided that I should return as a tourist, and not as a correspondent. Going back as a reporter would impose the complex difficulties of accreditation with the Soviet Press Department and, after all, I could write my impressions upon my return to London. So, through a British travel agency I applied for two tourist visas for a stay of six weeks. This seemed long enough. I asked to go into Russia by train and to leave by plane.

I received a reply within a few days. The visas would be granted, but the Soviet consul wanted to see my wife and asked that she bring along her old Soviet passport. Somehow that had a sinister ring.

"I don't know what the passport business is all about," I said to Tamara, "but you'd better go and see."

Since she had become an American through naturalization in a federal court in my home state of Alabama, she had, quite obviously, retired her Soviet passport and it was now out of date. We dug it out of a trunk, red as the ruby stars above the Kremlin's towers. It lay among the bundle of old Moscow papers, documents and tattered invitations to Moscow diplomatic parties.

Tamara clutched the passport and said, "Remember when I finally got this, got it with the exit visa in it? Remember all those years of waiting . . . ?" Her voice trailed off and she looked away. "Just seeing it again gives me a little shudder."

Before our marriage in 1943, Tamara Kolb-Chernashova had been a student. From the age of eight until I came on the scene, she was enrolled at Moscow's Bolshoi Theatre Ballet School. Several months after the beginning of our association, Stalin's political police arrested her for associating with me, a foreigner, whose country, incidentally, happened to be pouring millions of dollars worth of lend-lease equipment into the Soviet Union. But a foreigner was a foreigner and hence dangerous to citizens of a state building Communism. Banished from her mother's home and from Moscow she was lost to me forever, I feared. Then my friend, the late Wendell Willkie, appealed to Stalin and because of his appeal Tamara's banishment ended and she was allowed to return to her home and marry me. That is part of another story but it does emphasize, I think, her understandable fear of Soviet officials, especially when they want to examine old documents.

The consul in London was all smiles, however, and reassurance. Yes, he knew Tamara was now an American. No, there would be no difficulties about recognition of her United States passport.

Then why did he want to see her old Soviet passport?

"Ah," said he, "we're thinking of you. Why don't you have your Soviet passport brought up to date?"

"But I now travel on an American passport."

"Of course you do." This with more smiles. "But why not have two passports, an American passport and a Soviet passport?"

"Why should I?"

"Well—," the smile broadened. "We are thinking of you. You know how it is with the American Government. Sometimes the American Government can be rather beastly towards Soviet citizens, whether they have an American passport or not. With a Soviet passport, active and up to date, you could always rely on us for assistance. You could count on us for help."

Very politely, Tamara thanked him for his thoughtfulness and added, "If it's all right with you, I think I'd better think over your offer."

"Of course. There's no hurry at all. You may travel to Moscow on your American passport and you can come back to London on it. Then later, you can drop around and see us and receive your Soviet passport."

Tamara thanked him and gave him a special smile. I know that smile. It can be as chilly as a March wind off eastern Siberia's Lake Baikal.

"And tell your husband his visa is also ready."

"You are very kind."

"*Pozhalasta.*"

With the question of visas settled, our departure date was set for January twenty-second.

Once before I unsuspectingly put the Iron Curtain between myself and my children. On that occasion I had left them in Moscow with my wife, while I took an imperative business trip to New York. Now it was the other way around: I was going to Russia and leaving three children in England.

That first separation almost ended in tragedy. Due to the perversity of the Soviet Government, it took me eight months to get back to my family. I might never have done it but for a resolute stand taken by the State Department, which flatly refused to allow any additional Russian journalists to work in the United States until I had been given a visa to re-enter the U.S.S.R. The Moscow authorities at the time wanted to send two new correspondents to Washington, so I got my visa. Being kept apart was an ordeal for us all, and my wife and daughters all but convinced themselves that they would never see me again. The memory of those terrible months from October 1950 to May 1951 was very much with me, as they were with my wife, as we prepared to leave for Moscow on a dark snowy night in late January 1963.

Farewells *are* like dying a little, and we all died a bit as we said our good-byes. I have never parted from my children for any length of time without feeling guilty. I suppose this is because I sense their fundamental insecurity stemming from once being Cold War casualties; and from being dual nationals with a Russian mother and an American father and having spent their formative years in a country ruled for a period by a near madman. Yet surely our youngest, Natasha, born in London in 1957, could not be affected by something brought on years before in Moscow. Or could she? At parting there were no tears, but I thought I saw accusation in their sad eyes as we kissed for what we realized would be the last time for six weeks or more. In our hearts, Tamara and I were acutely aware that with bad luck the separation could be longer. I think they sensed our poorly disguised uneasiness.

"God of mine," gasped Tamara in Russian as we swept away from our house to spend the night in a London hotel in order to make a train departure early the following morning, "God of mine, I'm not sure I can go through this."

I took her hand and told her as reassuringly as I was able that she could call off the whole thing any time she wanted to.

"Either way," she said, "I'd never forgive myself. For ten years I've promised Mama that I'd come back and see her. Now this, the pain of parting and . . ."

"You don't have to say it. I know."

"Hoaney, I won't have any trouble getting back to the children, will I?" she asked for what must have been the twelfth time.

"No. If I thought there would be, I wouldn't let you go."

"I know you wouldn't."

Britain was in the grip of its coldest weather for a century. The Sussex and Surrey countrysides, deep in snow and swept this night by a howling gale, looked far more like Russia than temperate southeast England.

Mother to the end, Tamara next inquired of me for perhaps the tenth time if I thought the children would be all right on their own.

"Vicki will see to everything," I told her. "She's a big girl now."

Vicki was eighteen. Susanna was soon to be thirteen, and Natasha was just under six.

"Eighteen isn't very old when you have to be big sister, mother and father," said Tamara.

"When you were eighteen, you were becoming a mother."

"I was different. I was a Russian girl used to hard times and responsibility."

I reminded her that our neighbors, Dr. and Mrs. Francis Briggs, had generously offered to look in every day.

"And there's Mr. White," I added.

Mr. White was George White, gardener, carpenter, handyman, philosopher, tough and wiry at seventy-two. His first job in life, at the age of sixteen, had been as a birdfrightener at one shilling (14 cents) a week, in his bleak native county of Norfolk, a start in life that causes him periodically to observe with some feeling that he does not like to be reminded of England's good old days.

"Ah, yes," smiled Tamara. "How good of them all. What nice people are the English, especially to two funny foreigners like you and me."

Another English friend, Annette Tute, had fixed us up with a highly pleasant accommodation in one of London's new hotels, the Carlton Tower, an American-owned hostelry that operates on the theory that its guests are not amused at the prospect of freezing to death in drafty, poorly heated rooms. Accordingly, the central heating was on full force and the room temperature must have been about eighty when we went to bed.

I was up at six o'clock the following morning, for I was to appear on the British Broadcasting Corporation's amusing and erudite early morning program, "Today."

Arctic blasts blew down the London streets and as I was unable to locate a taxi I walked the mile or more to Broadcasting House. There I found John Baptiste De Manio, the program's generally genial but sometimes terrible tempered master of ceremonies, cursing the weather and looking as he always does, more English than any Englishman I know; yet Jack's father was Italian and his mother Polish. Jack and many others like him fought valiantly in the last war as British officers and soldiers.

In the studio I met for the first time Genrik Trofimenko, Moscow Radio's London correspondent, a pleasant young man with a pointed nose beneath a large pair of black rimmed spectacles, eyes that looked like two shiny buttons afloat in pudding basins, black wavy hair, parted in the middle with identical spiky tufts that shot upward on either side of his forehead, giving him the appearance of having a pair of short horns. Mr. Trofimenko was there to interview me.

It had been a long time since I had been interviewed by a

semi-official Russian, and a Moscow Radio man stationed in a foreign country is all of that. My last questioning by a citizen of the Soviet state had been in Moscow, by one of the stern-faced chieftains of the Foreign Minister's Press Department. The interrogation concerned one of my frequent brushes with the Moscow Militia for driving a car without a Soviet driving license. Despite the fact that I had driven automobiles consistently since the age of fourteen, and held permits from three American states and four European countries in addition to an international driving license, I could never pass the Russian test. They faulted me the fourth and final time because I was unable to give them the name in Russian of the large valve in a carburettor. I do not know what it is called in English, much less Russian.

"There have been many changes since you were in the Soviet Union," began Mr. Trofimenko. "In fact, the only things that haven't changed are the Russian winters and the hospitality of the Russian people."

"Those are two things that I think will never change," said I. "When I lived in Russia and the Cold War reached its most frigid depth, I was consistently treated with kindness by the Russian people. I emphasize, the Russian *people*."

"Why are you going back?"

"For a variety of reasons." I mentioned the anniversaries of Stalin's death and the Stalingrad victory, and added that as I had been in the U.S.S.R. for the original events I would like to be there all these years afterwards.

"Why are you going at such a cold time of the year?"

I thought my answer had covered that, but I added, "To get warm," and pointed out that since Boxing Day (December twenty-sixth) the maximum temperatures in Moscow had, on at least four days, been warmer than they had been in London.

In a more serious voice I said that I too believed great changes had taken place in Russia—changes that might well affect the lives of our children and our children's children, and that I was tremendously curious about them.

"I'm going back for sentimental reasons too," I stated.

"Sentimental about Russia?" broke in De Manio.

"Ah yes, you *can* be, you know. I had many friends there. A large number of them were arrested by Mr. Stalin and Mr. Beria, but I have heard that many of them have been liberated by Stalin's successors. I'd like to see them. Also, I had some of the best times of my life in Moscow and in so doing I collected some monumental hangovers."

"Did you ever see Stalin?"

"Many times."

"Did you ever interview him?"

"Yes, once."

"Did you cover his funeral?"

"Oh, yes."

"If the people hated Stalin, then why did so many of them go down to see his body when it lay in state in Moscow?" This was from De Manio.

"To make sure for themselves that he was dead."

Pause.

"What was your most intimate experience with Stalin?"

"Getting his permission to marry. And then there was a time at an embassy dinner."

"What was that?"

"I was standing at the bottom of the steps when he entered the British Embassy. He must have thought I was the butler, for he handed me his cap."

"Did you take it?"

"No. It was the worst boob of my journalistic career. Instead of taking it from him, I backed away."

"What was your first reaction, when you learned that Stalin had suffered a heart attack?"

"I'm afraid my first reaction was not a very Christian one. I had always told my wife that the only way we would ever be allowed to leave the Soviet Union would be when Stalin died, and consequently on that fateful early March morning in 1953, when I was informed that he was ill, my reaction was—'Well, I hope it's nothing trivial.' "

That ended the interview.

Outside Broadcasting House, Tamara and a chauffeur were waiting in a car piled high with luggage. We drove through thick traffic to London's Liverpool Street Railway Station to board the train for Harwich and then the boat for the Hook of Holland.

At the railway station we found British Railways running true to form.

"We must apologize for the boat train to Harwich being late," said a voice over the loud speakers. "The delay is due to a fault with the locomotive. It is being put right."

To my surprise I found Eddie Worth, a photographer from my London office, waiting on the cold platform, camera in hand.

"Why are you here?" I asked. "Somebody arriving?"

"No. Somebody's departing."

"Who?"

"You and Mrs. Gilmore."

"You don't want our picture."

"Yes I do."

The wheel had truly turned full cycle. Twenty-three years ago, this same Eddie Worth had been on the platform at London's King's Cross Railway Station to take a photograph of me as I left to join a not-nearly-secret-enough-for-my-liking convoy to Russia, starting from Greenock, Scotland.

"Newspapermen aren't news," I said.

"They would be," said Eddie, "if they didn't come back."

2. A Glass of *Chai*

With great wastes of snow and ice on either side of the tracks as far as one could see, travelling to Harwich was riding across the steppe of continental Russia in the dead of winter and it was not surprising to find the River Stour at Harwich clogged with ice cakes and frozen solid near the shore. I speculated whether my friend Randolph Churchill was snowbound at his country home in nearby East Bergholt.

We boarded the waiting Dutch steamer *Wilhelmina* and discovered we were a total of only eight passengers in first-class and even fewer in second. The weather being what it was, a steward commented that the crew was surprised to find anyone coming aboard. "It's a poor time," he added as if he were giving me good advice, "to go any place."

In more than thirty years of crossing the North Sea I never experienced a passage as calm as this, and certainly one that took place in such privacy. We were only seven paying passengers, I soon learned, for one of the eight turned out to be a young woman employed by the Netherlands Bureau of Tourism, or something such.

"Excuse me," she said as I stood near the bar, "but would you mind answering a few questions?"

"Of course not, Madam."

"First of all, we want to know why you're making this journey."

For a moment I was seized with the staggering thought that logical Dutchmen in some government department had dispatched her abroad, convinced that only dangerous lunatics would negotiate the North Sea under such extreme climatic conditions and that it would be in the interest of public safety to track them down.

"How do you mean, 'making this journey'?" I asked.

"Is it for business or pleasure?"

"Pleasure on a day like this?"

"It could be."

"Well, it's not."

"Then it's for business?"

"Yes, business."

She wrote something in a large black book.

"Are you alone or accompanied?"

"Accompanied," I replied, nodding towards Tamara.

"Your daughter?"

"My wife," I replied becoming more rattled with every question. She looked as if she did not believe me.

"Where are you travelling from?"

"A place called East Grinstead in Sussex."

"Nationality English?"

"Nationality American."

"Destination?"

"Moscow."

"Moscow?" This rocked her.

"I hope you'll excuse me, but what's this all about?"

"We carry out spot checks for the records. We check every tenth person. That will be all. Thank you very much."

She gave Tamara a long look and then stared me up and down.

"Young for her age," I said.

"Pardon, please?"

"I said she's young for her age."

"We are not interested in ages—" She backed off and disappeared around a corner, an apprehensive look on her face, I thought. I was sure she thought I was crazy and I vaguely expected trouble when we landed.

In addition to the cold, the day was blue and beautiful and a fireball sun slunk down the watery western horizon as the *Wilhelmina* nosed into the Hook of Holland shouldering ice blocks out of the way.

With so few passengers, the customs and immigration men eased us through in a couple of minutes. A most helpful American Express Company Dutchman, expecting to meet God knows whom, informed me when I asked that the Moscow Pullman had failed to arrive.

"But we were assured it would be here."

"With Russians you can never be sure of anything."

"What do we do?"

"That train," he said, motioning to one drawn up near the customs shed, "will take you to the German frontier. You may find the Russian car there. It often is."

"Quaint."

"Pardon me?"

"I said this is a bad way to start to Moscow."

Assisted by a pair of broad-shouldered porters, I got our luggage onto the Dutch train, offered the American Express man a tip, which he refused, paid the porters and joined Tamara in a spacious, clean and comfortable compartment.

"This train does connect with the Russian Pullman, doesn't it?" I asked the conductor.

"Oh yes. You'll probably find it at Oldenzal."

"Where's Oldenzal?"

"On the German frontier. I hope the Russian car will be there. Very often it is."

"And if it isn't?"

He shrugged his shoulders. "I expect you'll find it."

The train slowly pulled away in the direction of Rotterdam, quickly gathered speed and we began flying across the flat countryside, the locomotive giving out a baritone blast every three or four minutes. How different, I thought, from the high-pitched, effeminate tooting of British railway engines.

As we thundered towards Germany we decided it was time for food. The dining car was empty except for two stewards. Enjoying super-service, for both of them insisted on serving us, we had soup, omelet, roast chicken and a chateau-bottled wine. We sat there enjoying our meal immensely, watching the bare trees, silhouetted against the wintry sky, fly by. Tamara suddenly turned away from the window. "Hoaney, there's still time for me to turn back."

I was alarmed but I hope I did not show it.

"Turn back?" I said as casually as I could. "Of course you can, darling, and if you feel you should, well, just say so. That's all you have to do."

"Oh," she sighed, "I'm just being silly. I'm sorry."

"I know how you feel, and I don't want you to go on if you don't want to."

"I do want to. I just wanted to hear you reassure me." Leaning across the table, she kissed my cheek. A few minutes later the conductor entered the diner and announced that Oldenzal would be our second stop.

"Dress warm," he cautioned, "it's very cold outside."

Situated in the midst of the Dutch nowhere, the railway station at Oldenzal obviously was a long distance from the town proper and it presented a lonely and depressing scene. Heavy snow was falling and the old-fashioned gas-lamps at the top of tall iron standards cast a yellow and melancholy gloom over the deserted platform.

"No porters, I'm afraid," commented the conductor.

"I'm not so much worried about porters as I am about that Russian car," I said.

"Oh that. It's here. See?" He pointed into the snowstorm. I could see nothing but snow.

"Well," said the conductor, "as there are no porters and you have a heavy load I'll help you."

"That's very kind."

"I'm getting off here. I live here."

"Then I'm sure you want to be off to your home."

"No, no." He put down a small suitcase and energetically assisted me in wrestling our bags and boxes from the train to the platform.

"I'm going to look for that Moscow car," announced Tamara, marching into the snowflakes.

"Wait here beside your luggage," said the conductor as he disappeared in the opposite direction.

Standing there alone, I peered through the snow and dusk at the flat countryside and marvelled at the fact that here in Holland—next to Monaco the most thickly populated country in Europe—there could be a place as isolated as the railroad station at Oldenzal. As my eyes accustomed themselves to the lamplit and snowy gloom, I picked out a few weak lights flickering in the distance.

The Dutchman had found a hand trolley which we quickly loaded, and with my pushing and his pulling, we went off in the direction of what he promised was the waiting railway carriage. A hundred yards down the platform, it suddenly appeared in the swirling snow. I saw alongside the car those familiar initials with which I had lived for twelve years—C.C.C.P. In the Russian alphabet, they stand for Union of Soviet Socialist Republics. I smiled as I recalled how, many years before, an extremely well known American foreign correspondent, a man whose name became a household word during the last war, visited the Soviet Union for the first time and, in cabling back his breathless first dispatch, commented that the Communist Party dominated life to such a degree that it even plastered the sides of locomotives and railway carriages with C.C.C.P., which he explained stood for "Central Committee of the Communist Party."

He was, of course, unaware that in the Cyrillic alphabet C is what we know as the Latin S, and P is its R.

I also remembered how I too had suffered from ignorance and alphabet-trouble during my first weeks in Moscow. Above every restaurant I had noted the word РЕСТОРАН and tiring of hotel food, I one day suggested to my secretary-interpreter that I would be pleased if she would join me in a good meal at a pectopah.

"A what?" she asked in astonishment.

"A pectopah," I told her.

"I don't know what that is in any language," she said.

"Come on now," I said, pointing through the office window of the Metropole Hotel, "there it is over that restaurant door—РЕСТОРАН."

Very patiently she explained that РЕСТОРАН was RESTORAN or restaurant, and added, "Meester Geelmor, if you find it impossible to study our language, the least you can do is learn the alphabet."

As this flashed through my mind I heard a Slavic explosion up ahead. Moving in closer I saw Tamara banging on the C.C.C.P.'s glass door and calling out "Open up!" in her native language. The door then flew open and a pair of unmistakably Russian faces appeared.

Seeing Tamara, one of them quickly crossed himself and exclaimed, "God of mine, it's Anna Karenina!"

Dressed in her fur coat, a Cossack style fur hat, and soft black leather boots that reached her knees, Tamara did indeed resemble Tolstoy's tragic heroine who had ended her life at just such a railway station as the one at Oldenzal.

"No, I'm not," said Tamara rather crossly, "and I'd be obliged if you and your *tovarich* would get out here and help my husband and this gentleman get our baggage aboard your car."

The two Russian porters, or *provodniki* as they are called, continued to stare, apparently unable to adjust themselves to this Russian-looking and Russian-speaking woman material-

izing in a snowstorm on a lonely gas-lit railway platform on
the Netherlands-German frontier.

"You shouldn't be here," said one of the attendants.
"They told us no one would be getting on here."

"Well, we are here and you better do something about
us. I'm tired of standing in this snow. We're on our way to
Moscow."

"They told us no one would be here," the elder of the
provodniki repeated.

"But we are here!" shouted Tamara. "Why argue with
life?"

With a whoop of loud laughter, they tumbled outside and
tackled our luggage.

"What a cold Russian welcome," chided Tamara.

"Just you wait a bit," one of them came back. "*Chai* is
ready."

I produced the tickets for our compartment, excused
myself, and left the car to thank and tip the kind Dutch
conductor. Back inside the car I found that Tamara and
the two attendants were now in animated and good-humored
conversation.

From my accent—and I must be one of the few persons
in the world who speak Russian with an Alabama flatlands
accent—the *provodniki* knew instantly that I was a foreigner,
but they proclaimed that they were unable to understand
how my wife conversed in their language so perfectly.
Being Russian (and therefore mysterious and complex of
character), she let them guess.

As we were settling down in our compartment, a loud
noise echoed through the car and this was accompanied
by a violent lurch of the carriage. We were, I assumed,
being coupled to a train outside in the snowy waste. Ten
minutes later we were rolling eastward.

"Hoaney—"

"Not again?"

"Yes. I could still do it."

"Do what?"

"Get off and go back to the children. We're in West Germany not East Germany." This time, however, she made her declaration with a smile, rather bravely I thought, joking about her deep-seated fear.

I pointed to the emergency cord. "Want me to pull it?"

"No. I'll be all right."

Like a vaudeville turn, the *provodniki* stuck their heads into our compartment.

"I'm Sasha," said one.

"I'm Nikolai," said the other.

They looked at us wedged between our pile of luggage. "This won't do," said Sasha shaking his head. "You're too crowded. You need more room."

So saying, he and his helper pitched in, removed the portable wall that separated our compartment from the one adjoining and re-arranged our bags and boxes.

"Now you'll both have a lower berth and plenty of space to move around in."

"That's splendid," I said, "but I have tickets for only one compartment."

"*Nitchevo*," laughed Sasha, "who cares?"

I knew I was back among the Russian people.

Chai, steaming hot in tall glasses with stainless steel holders, decorated (if that is the word) with mass-produced machine-stamped replicas of the Kremlin's clock tower, and served with large slices of lemon—such tea is one of the world's best drinks. Nikolai brought it to us in tip-toed reverence, almost as an offering.

As he and Sasha seemed to have nothing to do but serve us, we insisted they sit down and join us in *chai* drinking.

The Pullman was beautifully sprung and easy riding and when I commented on this Sasha said, "All a matter of good shock-absorbers."

"I hope your restaurant car is as good as this one," I told him.

e it on condition that they'll join us here for

pted and said good night.

in Tamara's eyes.

ing wrong?"

well . . . it's the natural kindness of simple

le."

greed, "and yet some others are such bastards."

he simple Russian people. With some petty

perhaps yes."

at she was right.

tened at going back?"

tle."

re, if you're really and truly worried about it; if

ou shouldn't go through with it; if you've got

doubt, then tell me and you can get off the train

even Warsaw. As you know, the AP has offices

es. I'll call them—"

you, but I wouldn't miss this trip for anything.

how I want to see Mama and Zina and Vovo. As

erything's going to be all right, but—"

at?"

up a pair of crossed fingers. "I wonder how long

them crossed?"

a rough, tough Russian," I told her, "and you're

'd have to be to be married to me as long as you

w a pillow at me. It had been a long day.

"It will be—when they put one on."

"Put one on! You mean there's no Russian dining-car on this train?"

"No Russian, no German, no Polish. There's no restaurant car at all."

This was a serious matter and my face showed my alarm, for Nikolai asked, "What's the matter? You brought food, didn't you?"

I had been away from Russia so long I had forgotten that in taking a train journey of more than two hundred miles the traveller must stock himself with bread, butter, cold meat, cheese, sugar and hard boiled eggs.

"I'm afraid we brought nothing in the way of food."

"*Nitchevo*," said Sasha, "we've got plenty for us all."

"But we can't take your food. We'll buy something along the way."

He looked at his watch. "I'm afraid it's too late for the buffets in West Germany."

"Then we'll get something from one of the station buffets tomorrow morning."

The *provodniki* shook their heads. "In East Germany," said one of them, "you'll find nothing." "Don't worry," they chorused. "Would you like something now?" asked Nikolai. "I'll go get it."

"Thank you, no. We've already had dinner, but sit down, and let's have a drink."

Digging into one of my bags, I drew out a bottle of whisky and one of gin. Sasha and Nikolai looked on approvingly.

"I've heard of visky," said one of them, "but I've never tasted it."

"Help yourself."

We had a round and then Tamara poured again and again until both bottles were empty. Remembering how poorly the Russians I had known in the past drank spirits, I feared the worst, but things had changed. More to the point, our *provodniki* were obviously prodigious topers for neither showed the slightest sign of intoxication.

"I can't understand about you," said Sasha. "You both have American passports." He had seen them, for we had produced them at the German frontier. "And you, *gospodin*, speak Russian with a heavy accent, while you, Mahdom, have no accent at all."

"We've had hundreds of foreigners on this car," said Nikolai, whom by this time we were calling Kolya, the diminutive of the more formal Nikolai, "and you Mah-dom, speak Russian better than any foreigner I've ever heard. I don't understand how you do it."

"My parents were Russian," said Tamara.

"But still."

"Oh, go on and tell them," I said. "It'll save trouble."

Briefly, Tamara filled them in on her background.

"Wait a minute," she said as she reached for her handbag, "I want to show you something."

"I knew it," I laughed.

"Knew what?" she asked.

"It's photograph time."

"Of course."

Get two Russians together on a train, and sooner or later one of them is going to reach for his photographs—pictures of his children, his wife, and often his parents and grandparents.

As the attendants exclaimed over the photographs of our children, I took stock of the situation. In consuming the contents of the bottles of whisky and gin I had done my part, yet I knew I was not tight. Still, I had a sensation of gliding along rather than rolling along a track. I commented on it.

"It's those Russian springs we're riding on," said Sasha.

Before the Russians could make *sputniks* they understood the secret of manufacturing automobile springs. They made them of desperate necessity, for I have never been in a

Soviet city that did
streets and it takes go
Aside from the highw
roads approximate th
forty years ago. Go
and the welfare of th
would be a nation of

"By the way," I
car would at some tim
this take place?"

"Let's see," said Sa
26 hours from now, w
knew, was the first Sov

"Still worried about

"Yes, I'm worried t
food."

I recalled to myself
It had lasted twenty-on
angel with food for six
cow, but we got divert
on that trip. Instead, we
the Ural mountains into
hind the Urals, and wes
of Samara, re-named Ku
Tonight, as I once again
self that if I had previou
with food for only six, I
Litovsk only twenty-six

"We must leave you,
and you must have some

After profuse handsha
departed. Five minutes la
tray high with brow
cheese sweet cakes.

"If we can't accep
we'll hurt

"Then
breakfast.

They ac
I saw tea
"Is som
"It's . .
Russian p
"Yes,"
"Never
bureaucra
I agreed
"Still fr
"Just a
"Look
you think
the slight
in Berlin,
in both pl
"Than
You know
you say,
"But w
She hel
I can keep
"You'r
brave. Y
have."
She th

3. Starry Night
at Brest

Certain countries exude their own particular smells. In Britain, the aroma is one brought about by dampness, fried fish, spilled beer, tweeds in constant contact with cats, shoe polish, and the perfumed tobacco used for pipe-smoking. In France, it is the pungent mixture of scented women, garlic, dogs, wine, and the stale perspiration of Gallic bodies, caused not so much by uncleanliness as a low per capita proportion of bathrooms. The Italian emanation is much the same as the French—but with a subtle difference. It comes, no doubt, from longer hours of sunshine, an enormous intake of carbohydrates, a greater abundance of fragrant fruit, and the widespread use of hair oils and the oils of the olive. Across the United States the smell is of cigars (good and bad), popcorn, peanuts, hot dogs, hamburgers, fried onions, fresh newsprint, halitosis, flatulence, shaving lotions, strong coffee, a wide variety of disinfectants, and antiseptic females reeking of excessive ablutions.

The countries of Eastern Europe, with their Communist

and pseudo-Communist governments extend their conformity to an overall odor which is an effluvium of cabbage soup, black bread, kerosene, harsh soap and the conditions caused by the protracted lack of it, tobacco containing *mahorka*, sunflower seeds masticated and spat out on the floors, and overworked but undercleaned toilets. Therefore, at the instant of awakening on the morning of our second day's journey to Russia, I knew we were on the eastern side of the ideological divide, and it came as no surprise when a trio of heads from the German Democratic Republic appeared in the door beside my berth. Assuming they wished to see our passports, I said a greeting in bad German and handed over our documents.

My passport is really seven passports, all stitched together with the top one active and the others long expired. An American consul once suggested this was ostentation, but I told him it was nothing of the sort and that it had to do with much travel in Communist countries whose immigration and customs officials insist on knowing when and where you first entered their country, where and when you made your exit and all this for the second, third and so on times.

While a dark and intelligent-looking officer was going through my bundle, a particularly stupid-appearing underling swung open the door to Tamara's compartment. She was asleep and seeing this the dark officer hissed a savage sounding command whereupon the subordinate quickly closed my wife's door, looking as if he had been caught in the act of doing something uncultured. Everything was in order, for the officer returned our passports, saluted smartly, smiled and departed.

Shortly before the train reached Berlin's Ostbahnhof, we received another visitation, but this time they asked what kind of currency I was carrying. When I told them sterling and the amount, they too saluted and went away. Looking through the window, I saw the Ostbanhof was decorated in East German flags and there were many signs proclaiming the VI Parteitag, or Communist Party Congress, which I knew had only recently adjourned. As Mr. Khrushchev had been the guest of honor, I assumed he must be just ahead of us on his way back to Moscow via Poland.

"I hope," I said to Tamara who was beginning to surface, "that if Mr. Khrushchev is travelling on a train ahead of us he won't hold us up."

"He won't," she assured me. "He'll have a special train and it'll be going fast."

"But suppose he decides to get out and look at the crops. As a newspaperman I have accompanied him, you will remember, on tours of Britain, France and Austria. He always stops and looks at crops."

"Don't be silly. What crops could he look at in this snow?"

She was right. Even in Berlin the snow was deep.

As at last our train rumbled on eastward I remarked on the abundance of young or stunted pine trees that seemed to surround the old capital of Germany. As I entered Berlin with the Soviet Army years ago these dwarf trees made a vivid impression. Why do the trees grow so small around Berlin? I have asked this question of a dozen people and I have yet to receive a satisfactory answer.

The engineer sounded his whistle. Its tone was deeper than the baritone of the Dutch engine and I concluded that the farther east one goes the more masculine sound the locomotives, a theory that soon exploded when I heard the shrill toots of the Polish engines, which sounded almost as effeminate as those of Great Britain.

We reached Frankfurt on Oder at twelve minutes past eleven in the morning. Sasha, who had entered the compartment with *chai*, announced that as we were five minutes late, the dispatcher at Frankfurt would probably hold us up.

"They are insane on the subject of being on time," he said, "and even if you're two minutes behind schedule they'll detain you. They punish you this way."

He was correct. We were delayed by more than an hour. Looking through the window before our Frankfurt arrival, I noticed an acre or so of barracks standing behind high walls of barbed wire and armed guards stationed in goon boxes every seventy-five or one hundred yards. This prison camp was located at a town with the highly inappropriate name of Rosengarten.

The Polish frontier at last. Here the officials were just as polite as the East Germans, and the arguments and mix-ups I had anticipated did not materialize.

"How are you feeling?" I asked Tamara, the first time I had put the question to her since we had moved through the Iron Curtain.

"Fine. Where are we?"

"In Poland."

"One of my grandmothers was Polish. Her family name was Peculik."

"Interesting," I said.

"Not very, but it's conversation. I'm hungry."

"My God, I'd forgotten about breakfast. Let's call the boys."

I rang the *provodnik*'s bell. Both arrived.

"I saw you earlier this morning," said Kolya. "You were asleep. It was when I thought you called."

"You saw me asleep?"

"Yes, and you were the first person I saw this morning and when a woman is the first person you see in the morning, well, everything goes wrong for the whole day. That's why we were late getting into Frankfurt."

"An old gypsy tale," said Tamara. "I don't believe it, but I don't like being looked at by strange men when I'm sleeping."

"I'm not a strange man."

"No, I don't suppose you are, so let's have breakfast. It's your breakfast, by the way and my husband and I feel awful at taking it away from you."

"*Nitchevo.*"

So saying, we had what I thought was a superb breakfast.

All day long we rolled across the broad snow-covered waistline of Poland, a real steppe country with vast miles of flat plains, few trees, but dozens of hares, partridges and every so often a fox.

At Warsaw I turned on my transistor radio and listened to a Voice of America broadcast. It was described as Larry Leseur's first for the V.O.A. (Twenty-two years before, Larry and I had been roommates at the Grand Hotel in Kuibyshev, both reporting the Russian war effort from that flea-bitten hostelry on the high eastern bank of the Volga.) From Larry's broadcast we also heard that Mr. Khrushchev's special train was just ahead of us and that he would stop off in Warsaw to have talks with Mr. Gomulka, the Polish premier.

"So that's who's delayed us," said Sasha. "Might have known it would be a politician."

Accustomed to Soviet citizens standing mute, or bowing their heads in effusive agreement, or indulging in exaggerated praise at the mention of Joseph Stalin's name, I could hardly believe what I heard.

"Did you hear that?" I asked Tamara in English.

"I did, but why did you ask?"

"I just wanted to make sure I'm not going nuts."

When we reached the railway station at Warsaw, the Polish capital was only a splatter of dim lights in the distance. It was at this point that we learned through one of the *provodniki* that our British travel agency in London had miscalculated by a whole day our arrival time in Moscow. We were to arrive a full day ahead of what our printed itinerary called for.

"You can't blame that on Russian inefficiency," said Tamara defiantly.

"What time are we going to reach the Soviet frontier?" I asked.

Consulting his watch, Sasha replied, "About two o'clock in the morning, *gospodin*."

"Let's see. That about four hours from now."

"Better get some sleep, because we'll be a long time at Brest. That's where we change from narrow gauge to wide gauge. They take off all the wheels. You should watch them do it."

"I'll be too sleepy."

"Oh, you can't sleep. You'll have to get out for the customs and all that."

"Of course. We'll have to change our money and send a couple of telegrams. If we don't, there'll be no one to meet us in Moscow. They've been told we're getting in a day later than we are."

"Have a good time at Brest," said Kolya.

"What, at two o'clock in the morning?"

"Yes, a good time," spoke up Tamara. "I don't care what time it'll be, I'll be getting out on Russian soil."

"Russian snow," I told her.

"No matter, it'll be Russia."

Of all the figures of speech evolved by the American soldier in the Second World War, one of the most expressive was "sweating it out." To describe the inner nervousness, torment and anxiety before awesome events, few idioms are more graphic. Those final hours before we reached the Soviet Union were spent by me in my bunk sweating it out. As I remembered the agony and hopelessness of the Moscow years, when it appeared as if I would never succeed in freeing my family, logic gave way to doubt and despair.

In the berth across the way, Tamara was strangely silent. I was sure that she too was going through her private hell. It was a slowing down of the train that lifted me out of my black mood of uncertainty.

Out in the corridor I heard one of the *provodniki* say, "We've arrived," and I knew that meant that we were now in the U.S.S.R.

Switching on the light I saw from my watch that the time was fifteen minutes before two o'clock in the morning. Looking across, I saw that Tamara was wide awake.

"Congratulations," I called out with what I instantly realized was a forced cheerfulness.

"For what?"

"You're home."

"Da."

At this there was a knock on the door.

This was the moment I had been dreading—my first encounter after ten years with Soviet authority on Soviet territory.

"Come in," I said in Russian in a voice that was unusually flat.

The door slowly opened.

Three men stood there—an unsmiling officer and a pair of slab-faced soldiers, members of the frontier security force.

"Your passports."

I handed them over. The officer examined every page and this took several minutes.

"There's the visa," I said, pointing to it.

He looked up at me and nodded, then methodically, too methodically I thought, he smoothed down the pages and handed the passport over to one of the soldiers.

Over Tamara's passport he spent even more time.

"You," he said to her, "were born where?"

"In Moscow," answered Tamara.

"And you are an American citizen?"

"Yes."

I was getting fed up with this, but I said nothing. Why had he not asked me my place of birth? Why had he singled her out?

He pursed his lips, stared at her passport for a moment or two, shut it, examined the front and the back, pursed his lips again, re-opened the passport and passed it back to his subordinate.

"Now," he said, "please vacate your compartments."

I was not quite sure what was going to happen next. As we knew we would get out at Brest Litovsk, my wife and I were fully dressed.

We both rose and, with a quick glance at me, Tamara stepped through the door into the corridor. I followed. We stood there saying nothing as the officer and one of his men entered our compartments. The other stood there, his eyes on us. Inside, the officer gave an order. The soldier dropped to his knees and peered under both lower berths and slowly got to his feet and stood at attention.

Joining us in the corridor, the officer said, "Your documents will be returned to you in a few minutes." Then he smiled for the first time. "You will have about two hours here. Wouldn't you like to walk around outside? You are free to do so—after customs."

"When do we have the customs?"

The officer beckoned someone from the shadows at the far end of the car. A middle-aged civilian shuffled forward.

"Good morning," he said. "Anything to declare?"

Saluting, the officer and his men left us.

I told the customs official that I had a few presents for friends in Moscow. He seemed uninterested.

"And this large box," I said. "It contains photographic equipment for my Moscow office."

"What kind of photographic equipment?"

"Paper for printing pictures."

To my utter surprise he marked the box with a piece of chalk and said, "Cleared."

"*Valuta?*"

I handed over a currency declaration showing the amount of foreign money I was bringing into the country.

"No Soviet money?"

"None, but I shall need some."

"*Pozhalasta.* You will find someone just outside the car from Intourist. They'll be glad to assist you with your currency and anything else."

He folded my currency declaration and pointing to our bags asked, "These are all you have?"

"No more. This is the lot."

With a flick of his chalk he cleared them as casually and as quickly as he had the box of photographic paper.

"That's all," he said with a smile as he tipped his cap.

"*Spasibo.*"

"*Pozhalasta.*"

With that he departed. He had not opened a single piece of luggage.

"Whew!" I sighed.

"Things have changed," said Tamara in English.

"Yes, so far. Let's go outside. My stomach feels like my throat's been cut."

I led the way down the corridor. At the door stood Sasha and Kolya.

"Sure you don't want to watch them change the car trucks for wide-gauge track?" asked Sasha.

"I think not, thank you."

"Well, it'll all take about two hours. When the train's ready you'll find it over there, on the other side of the station."

"Our luggage, will it be safe?"

"I'll stay with it every moment."

"Thank you."

I stepped out into the clean cold air and helped Tamara on to the platform, covered with a thin layer of powdery snow. A dark-haired girl, her shoulders wrapped in a heavy shawl, approached us, a solitary figure on the long and wide platform.

"You are Mr. and Mrs. Gilmore?"

"Yes."

"I'm from Intourist. May I be of service?"

"Yes, thank you. I would like to change some money and send a telegram. Is this possible?"

"Of course. Please come this way."

She led us inside the big railway station at Brest Litovsk

and I encountered the old familiar Russian smell. In the waiting room was the scene I knew so well—sleeping figures, men, women and children, piled like dummies along the high-backed wooden benches, their luggage sprawled near them.

The Intourist girl led us to a cashier's cage where a grey-haired woman quickly changed several pounds into roubles.

"Is that all you want?" She seemed surprised that I took so little.

"I'll get the rest from my Moscow office." I felt she was due that explanation.

"*Pozhalasta.*"

"I'm afraid the restaurant is closed," said Miss Intourist as if reading my thoughts, "but there's a buffet. Down there, through the corridor and to your left."

"And my telegram?"

"Oh, yes, excuse me."

She took a blank form from the cashier and handed it to me. I wrote out a message to Preston Grover, the AP's chief of bureau in Moscow, one of a long line of correspondents who had succeeded me. Informing him that we were reaching the Soviet capital a day earlier than expected, I asked the girl when our train would reach Moscow and added this to the message.

"You are sure there's nothing more we can do for you?" asked the Intourist representative.

"I think not, thank you."

"It's been a pleasure. We hope you will enjoy your visit to our country, and if you think of anything else that I may assist you with, that is before your train leaves, then I shall be in here." She pointed to her office.

Shaking hands, we parted.

"What's happened to the old country?" whispered Tamara in English.

"What do you mean?"

"Why, everyone's so polite."

"Aren't they?"

At the buffet we bought two sandwiches, a sort of hamburger with a cold fried egg on top, one for Tamara and one for me. As repulsive as it looked, I was too hungry to care. Tamara also purchased about a pound of spiced sausage, our principal diet on our Russian Pullman.

"I'd have thought you'd be sick of that."

"I never tire of *kolbasa*."

"I see that you don't."

I bit into the cold meat and cold egg. Tamara watched for my reaction.

"It's good," I exclaimed, "it's real good."

"You've been in Russia too long."

I laughed. Her tension and mine seemed to have vanished.

"Come on," I suggested. "Let's walk around and see something of your country."

The Intourist girl re-appeared. "I hope you didn't find the buffet too bad," she said.

"No, not at all."

"If you would like some tea I can make you some in my office. It won't take long."

As much as we both would have appreciated the tea, we declined for we were aware that this girl had, in all probability, been awake all night waiting to meet the train and us, the only two foreigners aboard.

I appreciated once again the basic kindness of the Russian people. How helpful and kind they can be, with a dignity all their own.

"Well, good night again," she said with a smile, "and if you change your mind about the tea, I'm here."

We walked out of the station into the night and looked up at the vast dark sky from which a million stars flickered.

" '*This is the story of a starry night*,' " sang Tamara very softly. "Hoaney, do you remember that one?"

"Indeed I do. Like vodka, I appreciate Tchaikovsky best when I'm in Russia."

"I can appreciate him anywhere," said Tamara.

We stood there looking up at the stars.

"Do you know that old saying?" I asked her. "The one about the Kremlin and the stars?"

"You have so many sayings."

"It's not mine. It's an old Russian saying. It goes: 'The Kremlin stands over Moscow and over the Kremlin stand only the stars.'"

"I think I'm going to cry."

"Not for the Kremlin, Moscow and the stars?"

"Oh, no. I'm going to cry for poor Tchaikovsky."

"Why Tchaikovsky?"

"He was so very Russian."

"And so are you," I told her, "and I love you very dearly."

"Hoaney?"

"Yes."

"I feel very wonderful. I'm back. I've kept my promise to Mama."

4. The Lights
of Moscow

After eight hours of blissful sleep, I awakened in high good humor and found Tamara in the same mood. This pre-breakfast cheerfulness mystified me, for I am neither buoyant of spirit nor light of heart upon rising. Here I was flat on my back, my stomach occasionally twitching with twinges of indigestion (generated no doubt from that icy hamburger and frigid fried egg), my body rolling back and forth as our now all-Russian train hurtled through the Pripet Marshes. This physical state of affairs was hardly conducive to *bon naturel,* and yet I felt almost jubilant.

Had returning to Russia done it? I asked myself. Well, it was nice to be back, but in my heart I knew that the real test of Soviet sincerity would come six weeks later, when it was time for my Russian-born wife and me to board the London-bound plane. I realized that until we were airborne and over the frontier there was cause for anxiety. Yet, aware of this, I still felt marvelous.

Then all of a sudden I knew what had happened. Psychologically, I had trapped myself. I felt good because nothing unpleasant had happened on entering the U.S.S.R. No security man had kicked us around. No customs official had poked through our luggage and created difficulties. No immigration bureaucrat had questioned my wife's American citizenship.

In the past time and again I had seen a curious spirit of thankfulness take possession of people who had every reason to be furious at the injustices of Stalin's police state. On the most riduculous of trumped-up charges, wholly innocent men and women would be snatched from their homes, hustled to the Lubianka, the most dreaded place in Moscow, grilled and re-grilled and subjected to monstrous indignities and then, when defeated in spirit and body, confess to fantastic offenses of which they had been wrongly accused. Judgment was usually swift. Then, as the loved ones of these unfortunates recoiled in horror, the original sentence would be reduced. Ivan would not have to serve ten years, but eight! The reaction to this was always the same, not one of anger and revulsion at the over-all injustice, but thankfulness. "How kind, how very kind of our government to reduce Ivan's sentence," and their eyes would swell with tears.

In a way, here I was behaving in the same fashion. I felt good because some minor representatives of a central government in Moscow had treated two travellers with civility; two travellers, of course, who had entered the country as tourists, and paid rather dearly for it too.

"Still," said Tamara, "it was awfully nice of them. They could have been so different."

"Of course," said I, "and I much appreciate this change, but great Heavens, we shouldn't let ourselves become exuberant over what is regarded in most places as perfectly normal behavior."

"Now you're in a bad humor."

"No, I'm not and that's what's making me sore. I should

be in a bad humor, but no. I'm in great humor and I've no particular reason to be."

"Oh, well, I still think you're in bad humor when you should be appreciative and thankful, but come on, let's have breakfast. I'm starved."

I rang the bell for the *provodnik*.

"Is the restaurant car open?"

"Oh yes, *gospodin*. It's the next car forward."

As Tamara and I entered the diner, two waitresses in neat black dresses and white aprons sprang to their feet and greeted us with smiles.

"Any table you wish," said one.

"Are we too late for breakfast?" I asked.

"Too late?" she laughed. "You're never too late. If you want breakfast at four o'clock in the afternoon, then all you have to do is order it."

"But it's not four o'clock in the afternoon. It's eleven-twenty in the morning."

"If it were four o'clock in the afternoon," said the waitress, "you could still have breakfast. That's what we're here for. The chef and the waitresses are here to cook and serve you food."

"Thank you most kindly."

In English I said to Tamara, "How pleasant to be travelling in a country where the public transport is run for the benefit of the traveller and not for the comfort and convenience of the public transport employe."

I recalled how the London bus drivers and conductors had consistently rejected the proposal to put one-man buses on the London streets to give the public better service, and how often the busmen set arbitrary rules as to how long they would work and under what conditions, invariably putting their own comfort and convenience before that of the passenger.

We marvelled at the cleanliness of the tablecloths, the silver, the dishes and glasses, and the good humor of the waitresses. Ours actually seemed to enjoy serving us with fresh country eggs, ham and *blinchiki*, and coffee served hot. Between courses we stared through the wide windows at the miles of sunshine on snow, the islands of evergreens and the occasional sled that seemed to fly into the distant horizon.

The train stopped at Orsha and we studied the crowd milling around the station. Here was something new—people who smiled. In Stalin's Russia, one of the most frequent comments of foreigners visiting Moscow for the first time was, "The people you see on the streets—don't they ever smile?"

I kept repeating to myself that it was too quick to make judgments about a land I had not seen for a decade. However, I did have the feeling that some sort of magic had taken place. In those last ghastly months of the Stalin regime the whole population seemed oppressed by the man's paranoia, and an atmosphere of suspicion hung over the country like a corrosive fog choking up everything. From what I had seen so far, that fog had lifted.

Before leaving the dining-car we made arrangements to return at three o'clock for *blini*, those delicious, small and thin hot cakes that go so well with caviar and melted butter.

In the corridor of our car I was stopped by a well dressed man of middle years who asked in Russian, "Excuse me, but you are foreigners, aren't you?"

"Yes, we are Americans."

"This is your first visit to the Soviet Union?"

"No, I've been here before."

"Diplomat?"

"Anything but. I'm a correspondent."

"An interesting occupation. Is this your first trip back since the war?"

"I was here during the war, but I really didn't leave until the summer of nineteen fifty-three."

Since perfect strangers in Russia will sometimes introduce themselves and begin asking the most personal questions, I was prepared for inquiries about my age, marital status, and even more personal matters.

"My name is Abramov," he said.

"Mine's Gilmore."

"Have you noticed any changes since returning?"

"Well," I told him, "we only arrived this morning, but since you ask—yes, I think there are great changes, or so it seems to me. For one thing, people seem more friendly and to smile more."

"You are quite right. There has been a *bolshaia raznitza*," a big change. I was to hear this phrase very often.

"The officials at the frontier are so much nicer," I said. "At Brest I was surprised that no one told me what I could do and what I couldn't do, and I didn't see a single militiaman. When I left here every railway station seemed to have more militiamen than, well, time-tables. I haven't seen any soldiers either. They were all over the place in nineteen fifty-three."

"Nineteen fifty-three, you say. Of course, that was the year Stalin died."

"It certainly was."

"He was a bad man," he said shaking his head, "a very bad man."

This in itself was a revelation, for it was the first time in my experience that I had heard a sober Soviet citizen openly condemn Stalin. In their cups I had heard men and women criticize him, but not when they were sober.

"I must agree with you."

"Any logical man would."

"The Chinese," I could not resist saying, "don't seem to agree that he was a bad man."

"Some Chinese are not logical, but to get back to the Soviet Union, you will find great differences everywhere. We're free."

"Congratulations."

"I'm going in to have some tea. Won't you join me?"

Explaining that I had just eaten a large breakfast, I expressed my thanks and said I hoped we would talk again before we reached Moscow.

"It will be a pleasure," he said, "and perhaps your wife will join us."

While we had been talking, Tamara had gone to our compartments. Joining her there I was told that Sasha, the chief *provodnik*, had learned from someone—probably the officials at Brest who had seen my passport—that I was a correspondent and that the discovery upset him.

"Why?" I asked.

"You'd better ask him. Wait here, I'll call him."

Sasha's round face looked unusually serious as he entered.

"Are you a correspondent, *gospodin?*"

"I've never been anything else. I thought you knew."

"I thought you were a diplomat."

"Good God."

"Last summer," he said, "there was a West German correspondent in my car. He asked me a lot of questions and then he wrote some terrible things."

"You mean he quoted you? I won't quote you if you tell me not to."

"I don't mind that. He said our car wasn't clean and that the toilet stank and the tea was weak."

"Don't worry. I won't write anything bad about you."

"I'm not worried about myself. I don't want you to write anything bad about my car."

"I couldn't. It's a splendid, beautiful car and we love it, don't we, Tamara?"

"Of course we do."

Sasha beamed. "I wasn't worried, just concerned."

He left, saying he would be right back. Returning with a pen and paper he asked if I would write a testimonial about his car.

"Gladly."

What I jotted down sounded like the beginning of a love affair.

"Tamara Adamovna," he asked, "will you read what he has written?"

Tamara gave him a quick translation.

"Thank you very much, *gospodin*. You're kind."

"No, Sasha. It's you who's been kind."

"West German people are bad people."

"Don't judge them all by the one who said your toilet stank."

"You're right," he smiled. "Some of them are all right, I suppose."

The train slowed down.

"Smolensk," said Sasha.

"I'd like to get off. I haven't been here, let me see now, it must have been in nineteen forty-three, or forty-four with the Red Army. How long will we be here?"

"Just a few minutes. Don't go far."

Outside a warm sun was shining and the platform was crammed with people. Again, I was struck by the number of smiles and the laughter. We walked, as well as we could through the dense crowd, for ten or fifteen minutes and then the loud speakers called for attention.

The departure of our train—The Berlin-Moscow Express it was called—was announced in Russian, German, English and French. This was another surprise. In past years even in the big stations at Moscow and Leningrad departures were never given in anything but Russian.

Most Russians possess a well-developed sense of occasion and, although the propaganda of the Soviets is often clumsy in content, it is generally well timed and aimed at the propitious moment, large and small. Such was the case as our express neared Moscow. The loud speakers strung out along the corridors came alive with beloved tunes and melodies that would soften up the returning native and the romantic. (I confess to being a bit of the latter.) They took me back to the days when Tamara and I began going together, and reminded me vividly of so many gay and wonderful parties that began early and lasted till dawn. I was growing sentimental when I was brought back to reality with my wife's announcement that inasmuch as I had told the waitress we would be back for specially prepared *blini*, we had better go and get them.

Still smiling, the waitress—who had told us her name was Vera—said the *blini* were ready, the caviar cold and the butter warm. "Now what will you have to drink?" she asked.

"Vodka, of course. With *blini*, what else?"

"I'm sorry. We have no vodka."

"No vodka?"

"We have cognac."

"Cognac with *blini* and caviar? No thank you."

"Then, perhaps, some white wine?"

"I think that would be better, but what's happened? I've never been any place in Russia where I couldn't get vodka."

"Cognac is more cultured than vodka, *gospodin*."

"I see. Thank you. I'll take the white wine. I presume it's also cultured."

"It is." Her smile was so sweet and friendly I decided to let her and culture have their way.

The *blini* were marvelous and the caviar was just as it should be, large lashings of small grey eggs that did not cling together in a gooey mass.

Many more passengers must have boarded the train, for the dining-car was full. Outside, the skies were darkening and in late January night comes on fast in Russia. Thoroughly satisfied, as indeed was Tamara, I paid for the meal, overtipped Vera and told her farewell.

Next, I looked up Sasha and Kolya.

"Good-bye, friends," I told them. "You have made our return to Russia very pleasant. Now how much do I owe you for this extra compartment?"

"Nothing, *gospodin*. The car's only half full. The extra compartment was not needed. You owe us nothing."

I thanked him—and tipped them both, heavily.

"We must have at least one bottle left," I said. "Come, a farewell drink."

"*Gospodin?*" said Sasha as I poured out four stiff drinks, "*gospodin,* does America want war?"

"Of course not."

"See," said the chief *provodnik* turning to his assistant.

"Nobody wants war," said Kolya very solemnly.

Out in the corridor I heard our new found friend, Mr. Abramov, calling to us, "Come out here and see the lights of Moscow."

I consulted my watch. Set to Moscow time it showed six-thirty in the afternoon.

"It can't be," I said. "We're not due until seven thirty."

"Running early," commented Sasha.

"When did Russian trains start running early?" I demanded.

"After Stalin died," he answered.

"I think you're making a joke," I told him.

"I am," he said. "We can't blame everything on him, but he was a *svuloch* just the same."

Tamara and the *provodniki* joined Mr. Abramov. I was alone in the double compartment.

Tamara appeared in the doorway. I saw and understood her excitement. "Come, hoaney," she called. "You must see the lights. The new buildings. It's a whole new city."

"Just a moment and I'll be with you. I'm looking for something."

Mr. Abramov stuck his head in the door. "Moscow's not out that window," he said. "It's over on this side."

"What I'm looking for should be over—about right over there." I pointed through my window.

"What are you looking for?"

"The Hippodrome."

"God of mine," cried Tamara. "He's seeing one of the world's great capitals for the first time in ten years and what does he look for? A racetrack."

During my Moscow years I have been a constant customer of the old Tsarist racetrack, out off the Leningradsky Chausée, near that splendid pre-Revolutionary nightclub-cum-gypsies, the Yar. The fairly new Sovietsky Hotel stands on the site of the old Yar, where the sugar barons used to sing in the dawn with the gypsies. Of that era, the Hippodrome remains, a tattered reminder of the old days and one of the lushest and most corrupt societies of modern time. Living in Russia under the grim dictatorship of Joseph Stalin, I had to have escapes. Mine were going to the racetrack three times a week, reading that salubrious British magazine, *Country Life*, and playing in an American jazz band called "The Kremlin Krows," then "The Purged Pigeons" and finally, "Joe Commode and His Four Flushers."

Sighting the Hippodrome—a dark silhouette against the lights of the highway to Leningrad—I sighed and then joined the others in the corridors.

"Yes," I said, "Moscow's a pretty sight tonight."

At the Bylerussky Vauxhall there was, of course, no one to meet us. I had messaged my office that we were arriving at seven thirty and here we were, forty-five minutes ahead of schedule.

Fearing that her mother might spend endless hours waiting on the station platform for her, Tamara had sent no telegram to her family.

I hailed a pair of porters, dressed exactly as when I had left Russia, in thick padded jackets and baggy trousers stuffed into long felt boots called *valenki*.

"Where to, *gospodin?*"

"Intourist is supposed to meet us. Have you seen any of their representatives?"

"No. It's a big station, *gospodin*."

"All right, just take us inside to a telephone. It's cold out here."

Actually, it was not terribly cold. Nothing like so cold, in fact, as when we departed from London's draughty Liverpool Street Railway Station.

At the gates leading to the station proper and its waiting rooms, our porters sighted the station master.

"*Tovarich Commendant*," they called.

An individual with a long blue overcoat, a black fur hat and long mustaches smiled at me.

"What embassy?" he asked.

"I'm an American," I told him. "Have you seen anyone from Intourist?"

"They may be outside in the street in their cars, but it doesn't matter. We'll take care of you. Marina!"

A large, smiling woman with front teeth of gold, dressed in a semi-military jacket that I recognized as that of the Railways Corps, waddled over. She was large, padded all over and authoritative.

"*Tovarich Dejurnaya* (Comrade Duty Officer)," bellowed the Station Master, "take care of our guests."

Thanking the official, we followed the Duty Officer. She led us to a castlelike door. All that was missing was the moat and drawbridge. With a huge key she unlocked it and, inviting us to enter, led us to a large table in a room of gigantic proportions. While I asked the porters to wait with the luggage until I found someone from Intourist, Comrade Duty Office went to work on a battery of six or seven telephones, denouncing Intourist in asides to us. After a few minutes of this, well sprinkled with colorful invective, she found someone some place. As she told them what she thought of an outfit that would allow a pair of foreign guests to arrived in Moscow un-met, I looked about me, at the high ceiling and the wall adorned with enlarged photographic portraits of the nation's leaders.

How odd it was to be in Russia, among portraits of men in the Kremlin, and to find no likeness of Stalin glaring down on you.

"Who's missing?" I asked Tamara above the flood of

opprobrium *Tovarich Dejurnaya* was pouring into the telephone.

"Uncle Joe," she replied in English. "But you didn't expect to find him, did you?"

"No, I suppose not. Yet, in a way, it's like arriving in the Arctic and not seeing a polar bear."

"What do polar bears have to do with Stalin?"

"Let it go."

At last, the Duty Officer received assurances that a driver from Intourist would be arriving very soon to meet us.

"They thought you were getting in tomorrow," she said. "The idiots!"

"I sent them a telegram from Brest this morning, giving them the change in date."

"Typical of them," she boomed.

"Please," I asked, "what's this room we're in?"

"The Deputies' Hall."

It all came back to me. Years ago, I had interviewed the late Ernest Bevin, then British Foreign Secretary, in this room. Telling Tamara about it, I added, "Right at this table."

"You're not impressing me," she said.

There was a hammering on the big door. The Duty Officer opened it and in came Preston Grover, a friend of mine for twenty-eight years. He was a splendid sight and we exchanged the warmest of greetings.

"I'm sorry," he said, "your train is early."

I apologized and thanked him for showing up.

We expressed our appreciation to *Tovarich Dejurnaya*, paid off the porters and got into two cars, Tamara with Grover and I with most of the luggage in the AP's car. We roared off down Gorki Street, a thoroughfare that I knew well. A lot I saw was new, but there were many things I remembered as standing there when I left. In a few minutes the ruby-colored stars atop the Kremlin towers came into view and with them a dozen memories of the good and bad days.

We stopped in front of the National Hotel and from its spacious plate glass door rushed a trio of porters.

One of them stared at me as if I were a ghost.

"*Gospodin*," he cried. "It's you! After all these years."

"Vanya," I shouted, "you're still on the job."

"And you too," he said. "Come on inside and get warm."

5. "The Kremlin Krows"

Travel-hardened to delay—and the Soviet Union has no monopoly on this—I was not surprised to stand in the lobby of the National for about twenty minutes while a most helpful receptionist sorted us out. Finally we were escorted to Suite 428, consisting of a small foyer, a reception room resplendent with a Soviet Chippendale sofa, chairs and desk, a bright pleasant bedroom in Karelian birch, and a bathroom in Victorian porcelain and tile. Triumph of triumphs, the tub contained a plug, a luxury offered by few hotels in the U.S.S.R. ten years before. (Previously I never moved from Moscow without my portable plug.) Our bathroom had another innovation—toilet paper. During my previous residence in Russia, I had found toilet tissue in the Kremlin, the Metropole Hotel and the Hotel Moskva, usually only on special occasions, but nowhere else.

Our living-room and bedroom overlooked the roof of the hotel's north wing and a tremendous illuminated sign that adorned the office building of the Council of Ministers. In arresting block letters, the sign read "FORWARD TO THE VICTORY OF COMMUNISM."

Interrupting me as I gazed upon that sign with which we were to live for weeks, Tamara said, "And now, for something for which I've been waiting for ten years—seeing Mama."

As I knew this would be a very emotional meeting, I suggested she see her mother without me. Warning her against overdoing things, I urged Tamara to limit her visit to an hour or so.

"Tell her that the two of us will come to her tomorrow," I added.

Grover made his car and driver available and off went my wife with loads of presents and a heart full of love.

"When you come back, join us in the restaurant," I called out after her.

"Which restaurant?"

"The best one in town is this one," said Grover, "the restaurant in the National."

Located on the second floor, this restaurant gives the customers a spectacular view. You look out on Red Square, with Lenin's Tomb, the onion-domed and many-colored Church of St. Basil the Blessed, and the Kremlin itself.

Grover had reserved a table beside the plate glass window, which extends from floor to ceiling, and as I sat down I began behaving as if I were watching a tennis match, switching my eyes from Red Square to the restaurant's dance floor, back to the magnificent scene outside, and then once more to the dancers and the people at the tables.

Here was another change. Most of the clientele were Russians and young ones at that. All during the war and up until the time I left, foreigners made up the bulk of the patrons of the expensive Restaurant National, and the Russians who ventured inside were relatively rich factory managers, minor Soviet officials, and an occasional Red Army, Navy or Air Force officer. Tonight the accent was on youth, young men and women in their twenties and early thirties.

The doddering old waiters had disappeared and, for tonight at least, they had been replaced by a group of brash and not very efficient young waiters and waitresses.

At the far end of the room a six-piece band blasted away at Western numbers, but the biggest musical surprise was seeing a Soviet musician fingering an electric guitar while the whole outfit played Kurt Weill's "Mack the Knife."

This was Moscow's café society. The girls wore their hair either bouffant or bee-hive and two or three of them looked charming. While not elegantly turned out, it was the best dressed group of young people I had ever seen in the Soviet Union.

I watched the dancing with mounting interest. To my amazement I saw a couple dancing cheek-to-cheek. The majority of the girls were big-busted. I have always contended that Russian women either have the best breasts in the world or the best brassières. The Soviet female is a combination of bourgeois prudery and startling immodesty. In a novel I once wrote:

"Only reluctantly will she wear dresses showing the slightest breast cleavage. Yet she will go swimming in the nude. She will shrink from kissing in public, but more readily go to bed with someone she loves than many Continental girls, excluding perhaps Hungarians."

I noticed that the diners and dancers about me neither ate nor drank very much, which no doubt partially explained why so many of them could afford the steep prices of the National.

"What's become of vodka?" I asked my friend. "We couldn't get any on the restaurant car of our train, and I don't see much around this place."

I was told that in restaurants it was rationed to Soviet customers, but as always the degenerate foreigner, who is, of course, beyond Communist salvation, could buy as much as he could pay for.

Within a space of fifteen minutes, two fights started. Waiters broke them up, and a young man sitting behind me, who had managed to get drunk on something, shouted in a loud voice that he was unable to pay his bill. His friends placated the waiter by saying they would pay for him.

"All right," warned the waiter, "but he's not going to get any more cognac until he, or you, can pay up for what he's already drunk."

To myself I said that I wanted a much longer and much harder look at present day Soviet café society before I made up my mind about a number of things.

Grover and I ordered and quickly downed several small glasses of iced vodka. Then, after a while, Tamara joined us. She was full of smiles and radiantly happy at having seen her relatives.

"They all send you their warmest love," she told me, "and I'll tell you about them later. Right now, may I have a drink?" I knew she needed one, and more iced vodka was rolled in.

For the next thirty minutes or so, my wife was invited to dance by at least a dozen young men. This Soviet custom may be all right for the ladies, but it can be infuriating for their escorts, and I for one have never gotten used to it. I have operated on the theory that since I do not bother their girls, they should not bother mine. Alas, it seldom works and in a land where dancing with strangers from another table is an accepted form of behavior, one either has to submit or adopt devious tactics.

The girl can always refuse, of course, but this may create trouble and invite insults from the spurned male. I knew one dazzling English girl who bandaged an ankle before she dined out in a Russian restaurant (there are no night clubs). When approached, she would look sorrowful and stick out her leg, shapely even under the surgical dressing. This worked like a mystical charm until one evening, at the Moskva roof garden, she faked her best wounded look and pointed to the bandage. The young man who desired her as his dancing partner looked shocked, turned and rushed for the exit, reappearing in a few minutes with a doctor.

I once knew every head waiter in Moscow and a wink from me would bring them to my table on the run, and in the sternest of tones they would warn off all strangers. I don't know why it is, but the average Russian is easily intimidated by a man in evening dress and my head waiter friends who did not wear tail coats usually managed to be formidable enough in dinner jackets. As I did not know the head waiter in charge of the Restaurant National on the evening of our arrival in Moscow, my wife had an energetic if not gay time.

In desperation she begged off one young man, saying in Russian, *"Malchiki,* I'm exhausted. Please dance with your own ladies for a while."

"But I don't often have an opportunity of dancing with a foreign lady," he said, "especially one who speaks Russian so well."

"If it's talk you want," replied Tamara, "then please let's sit down to do it."

"Your cavaliers (he meant Grover and me) may not like my sitting with them."

This cavalier made no reply.

"Aloysha," shouted a red-haired girl from two tables away, "come back here where you belong."

She had not played the game, but she had been effective. Aloysha bowed deeply to Tamara, kissed her hand, glared at me—and departed.

"I'm sorry," I said, "for the ordeal."

"No ordeal at all," replied my wife. "I enjoyed it—up to a point. I was being truthful when I said I was tired."

She paused and then went on, "England is a man's world. After you've lived there for a while, you forget you're a woman. It takes a trip to Italy or France or Russia to restore your morale, all the wolf whistles, pinches and—" she gestured with both hands, "all this dancing."

We were joined by Robert and Eleonore Tuckman. Bob,

of my London office, was in Moscow doing a relief stint for the AP and brought along his beautiful and shapely German-born wife. After enthusiastic greetings, we returned to the subject of wolves, particularly the Soviet variety.

"At least," said Tamara, "they neither pinch nor bite."

"Only this evening at a cocktail party," said Eleonore, "at the Soviet Writers Club—well, one of them suggested that I leave my husband and marry him."

"How quaint." This from her husband.

When the evening had run a loud and gay course, Tuckman suggested we join him and his wife at the Metropole for a nightcap. Tamara agreed and, as I felt in need of air and exercise and liked both Tuckmans very much, the idea appealed to me too. Grover begged off, saying he had a full schedule ahead of him.

The Metropole is less than a quarter of a mile from the National and we walked it, along down Moscow's broad sidewalks swept clean of snow. Hundreds of times I had made this walk—past the Council of Ministers building, alongside the Hall of Columns, the former Noblemen's Club, the scene of many melodramatic events, from the purge trials to Stalin's funeral, and then on before the Bolshoi Theatre, and the Mali to the Metropole.

"Ah, Mother Metropole," said I, "where I spent so many years."

This hotel too had changed. It used to have a musty, dusty, old-fashioned charm, but someone had tried to tart it up. They had moved out the old solid furniture and replaced it with modern stuff. I knew the sumptuous but slightly frayed suite where my friends were living and some of its nice Chinese pieces were still intact.

We talked nonsense for an hour and then Tamara and I thanked our hosts and started back to our hotel. We took another route, going past what is said to be the world's first three-dimensional cinema, then by the perfume shop where years ago I once saw something advertised as "Stalin's Breath."

Reaching the big intersection, where the National stands on one corner and the Moskva on the other, we noticed that a subway had been built for pedestrians. Walking through it, I remarked, "This'll save a hundred lives a year." I have always held that the Russian peasant has never accepted the automobile, subconsciously, and for this reason he tends to walk out into roads, streets, avenues, highways and intersections, looking neither to the right nor left. At this busy intersection pedestrians—and a great many of them were peasants—were bowled over daily by onrushing cars, buses and trolleycars. I must have witnessed a half dozen deaths at this busy crossroads.

In the depth of this Russian winter we found our room suffocatingly hot and had to throw open the windows, but this brought us face to face with the glare of the sign on the government building across from us.

"FORWARD TO THE VICTORY OF COMMUNISM" it proclaimed in God knows how many kilowatts.

"Nuts to you," said I, drawing the curtains.

From the bathroom, "What did you say?"

"I was behaving like a Fascist beast."

"What's that?"

Quoting a Turkish diplomat I once knew, I said, "A Fascist beast is someone who puts the interests of his own country above those of the Soviet Union."

The fact of just being back in Moscow had, I suppose, exhausted us physically as well as emotionally. I am not sure when we would have awakened on that morning after our arrival had there not been a strident banging on the double doors of the foyer. I had completely forgotten that, before retiring, we had left a breakfast order with the fourth-floor *Dejurnaya*. Their posts are behind a desk facing the elevator on every floor of the National.

Staggering from a dreamless sleep, I reached the door and, expecting almost anything, flung it open. Before me stood a short, blond, very blue eyed, broadly smiling young waiter in a dark dinner jacket. In a voice like a top sergeant at roll-call, he announced his name as Viktor.

"I came as you ordered," he fairly shouted. "At exactly ten o'clock."

"I congratulate you on your punctuality."

"Wait," he said, "until you've tasted your eggs." This statement sounded more like a warning than a promise of goodies to come.

Viktor stood by, watching as I sampled.

"Splendid," I said. "In all of Russia I've never tasted a better pair. For one thing, they're not cooked in sunflower seed oil."

"Oh, no, *gospodin*. They've been fried in good Russian butter."

"As I told you, they are splendid. Did you cook them?"

"I did, in my little kitchen just up the corridor."

"And napkins," I went on, "it's nice to have such freshly laundered napkins."

"*Gospodin*, where do you think you are—in some provincial hotel in America?"

My smile told him he had scored.

"Things have changed since I was last here, Viktor."

Tamara entered through the bedroom door and, everything considered, she looked lovely. Greeting Viktor as well as me, she said, "I heard through the door that the eggs are excellent." She and the waiter then became involved in a lengthy discussion over the respective merits of white and brown eggs. They did not settle the matter. In any case, Viktor left after assuring us in his resolute manner that if there was ever anything we wanted, it would be his pleasure to serve it.

"I must say Viktor's a pleasant change from the old days."

"Look, we're going to start boring one another if we keep up this commentary on the changes."

"But so many things have changed. Don't you agree?"

"So far, yes."

The telephone rang. In Russia as elsewhere I leave the telephone answering to my wife. It was Tamara's sister Zina. I jumped to the phone and we exchanged long and fervent greetings. She relayed my Russian mother-in-law's invitation to visit the family that evening. I thanked her and said we greatly looked forward to the event, for that is what I knew it would be.

Tamara and I spent the remainder of the morning sorting out clothes to be laundered and suits and dresses to be pressed, this operation being supervised by a chambermaid called Luba, the diminutive of Lubov, a much favored first name. Incidentally, in the long Russian lexicon, Lubov is the only feminine Christian name I know of that does not end with the letter A.

As for Luba, all diminutives stopped with her name. She was enormous. Everything about her—face, neck, shoulders, bust, hips and legs—was large, and from her head to her immense ankles, bulging beneath the voluminous hem line of her tent-like dress, her figure seemed to grow progressively bigger, making her overall shape pyramidal. Encased in a light brown uniform, she gave me the impression of a giant sack of potatoes that had undergone a severe shaking with the heaviest potatoes by force of gravity sifting to the bottom. She looked like a child's Billiken toy, leaded at the base. I longed to tip her over, for I was sure she would spring back to an upright position. Luba was good-natured and gentle and during our stay she swamped us with kindness.

"*Gospodin*," she asked, "why is it that Mah-dom speaks so much better Russian than you do?"

"Because she's smarter than I am."

Luba thought this over for a moment. "No woman's smarter than a man," she said very solemnly.

"Are you married?" I asked.

"*Da.*"

"Is your husband smarter than you?"

"God of mine, yes. He's much smarter."

"You sound like a happily married woman."

"I am. But you two, you and Mah-dom, you look happy, and yet you say Mah-dom's smarter than you are."

"I say she's smarter than I am in Russian only."

"Were you ever frightened as a child, *gospodin?*"

"I think I was. Why?"

"Yes, that's it. You were frightened as a child and this had something to do with your accent."

Tamara has never understood my penchant for off-beat conversations with Russians.

"Luba," she interrupted, "please don't pay any attention to what he's saying. He's a very silly man. Anyhow, it's time for lunch." And then in English to me, "I simply cannot understand why you get involved in these stupid conversations."

"Russians are the only people I know who will keep such conversations going. It's like two poor tennis players. For them it's a minor triumph to get the ball across the net, and they keep batting the ball back and forth. Yes, Russians like Luba are conversational volleyers."

"Sometimes I think you're crazy."

At the dining-room door we were greeted by an old friend, Georgi V. Medvedev, maitre d'hotel of the Restaurant National. His greeting was effusive and he even bent low and kissed Tamara's hand with a nicely balanced flourish, an old world courtesy often encountered in the Soviet Union. After a long exchange over how many years we had known one another and the state of our respective healths, he led us to a table beside the window. Summoning two, not one, waitresses, he told them, "Bring them nothing but the best. They are old guests of ours."

It was my time to bow. Outside, it was snowing hard. At times the flakes were so thick they blotted out the view of the Kremlin buildings looming behind the little Alexandrovsky Park and the towering, crenelated, red-brick walls.

In the afternoon Tamara rested while I visited the United States Embassy for a reunion with a number of old friends. These included Ambassador Foy Kohler, who was old to the Moscow post but new to his job as ambassador; John M. McSweeney, the minister; and Richard T. Davies, Ken Kerst, Carroll Woods, Colonel Peter Urban and Robert German.

Kohler had established a weekly meeting with the American correspondents stationed in the Soviet capital. Before this meeting I saw the ambassador for a pleasant personal exchange about the old days and old Moscow friends. I do not know what causes the warm and firm free-masonry among people who have been together for any length of time in the Russian capital; it defies time and separation. Kohler appeared to be feeling his way along the diplomatically tricky Moscow course. A cautious and highly intelligent man, he is one of the best of our career officers. He was soon to leave Moscow for his first report to Washington. He said he had just called on Soviet Foreign Minister Andrei Gromyko, and speaking of his pending visit to the United States, he said it was his first since taking over the ambassadorial job three months previously.

"I asked Mr. Gromyko if he had a message that I might take back to Washington with me," said Kohler, "and he replied that he had none. I told him that should he have one—between then and the time of my departure—I would be glad to relay it." The ambassador paused. "He hasn't called me," he said.

I watched Kohler's face as he talked. In thirteen years he had changed very little. He was the same kindly man, with what a woman might call a sweet smile, and an unhurried way of talking in a deep resonant voice. In our talk I brought up the subject of changes since the days of Stalin, telling him I was astounded by what I had already seen. He agreed that the changes were many.

"Phyllis (Mrs. Kohler) and I have entertained more Russians in our home here in three months than all the ambassadors did during Stalin's time, excepting perhaps Bill Bullitt." William Christian Bullitt, the first United States ambassador to the Soviet Union, began his tour of duty in 1933.

At his meeting with the correspondents, Ambassador Kohler recalled that one of them had written that Khrushchev's son-in-law, A. I. Adzhubei, had fanned up a wind of change in journalism as the new editor of *Izvestia*.

"I can't agree with that," said Kohler.

"But he did for a while," came back one of the correspondents.

Somebody asked Kohler if he had yet called on Alexei N. Shepelin, Chairman of the new Control Commission. As the man in charge of state security, he is a successor of L. P. Beria. Some also think Shepelin, only 44, may be Khrushchev's successor.

"I haven't called yet," replied the ambassador. "but he's on my list."

I resisted an urge to say, "And I bet you're on his too."

Asked if he knew of any precedent for such enormous power to be vested in a job like Shepelin's, especially as the Soviet constitution did not seem to endow him with such authority, Kohler, with a wry smile, replied, "I think Eddy Gilmore will agree with me that Beria didn't seem to need any written constitutional authority."

After thirty-five minutes with our man in Moscow, I went in to see John McSweeney; this reunion too was warm and nostalgic. Then on to Colonel Peter Urban, onetime hot fiddle player in "The Kremlin Krows." This band was organized by George F. Kennan, when he was minister-counsellor in the Moscow Embassy during some chilly days of the Cold War. As I explained in an earlier book about Russia, the late Soviet Minister of Foreign Affairs, Andrei Vyshinsky, complained about the band's name. He thought it reflected disrespect towards the Soviet Government. We then became "The Purged Pigeons," but this took a great deal of explaining to new arrivals in the foreign diplomatic corps, so I changed it to "Joe Commode and His Four Flushers." Americans understood this obviously awful pun and asked no questions. It did not strike foreigners as anything unusual, so they pestered me no longer—but a lot of them did address me as Monsieur Commode.

Joe and his Flushers played for diplomatic dances and, since we played for free, you can imagine our popularity and continued success, especially when I point out that to hire a Russian dance band a host would have to spend the rouble equivalent of about one thousand dollars.

"You know," said Pete, who is now the Military Attaché in Moscow, "I was down at the American House the other night and damned if your drums aren't still there."

It was really the face of my bass drum that had offended Vyshinsky, for I had decorated it with a painting of the Kremlin's Spassky Tower, and painted in a covey of black crows circling it at dusk.

Later, during a large diplomatic reception on our return to Russia, ten years after the dissolution of "Joe Commode and His Four Flushers," Ambassador Kohler stopped me and said, "You know, I'd give anything to revive The Kremlin Krows. What we need is a good piano-player and, if the State Department will only send me one, we'll be on our way."

6. Reunion in Apartment 137

Three years before Stalin's death, Mr. Beria's political police put a stop to Tamara's family visiting my Moscow home. They called it "a dangerous house." I had been called a number of things in my life, but dangerous was something new. During the final years of my Soviet residence I saw neither my wife's mother, sister, brother nor any of her vast number of aunts, uncles and cousins, some of whom had become very dear to me. For their part, I think they looked upon me as a relative and friend.

On our final evening in Moscow, on a Monday in June, we decided that, as we were leaving the country, and Stalin was no more and the skids were under the police, a visit would compromise no one. It was our final visit to the two-roomed apartment that Tamara's mother shared with her two other children, Zina and Vovo. (My wife's father died when she was twenty months old.) My Russian mother-in-law is a gentle, sweet woman who looks far younger than her years. She is also very close to her children and, as we said farewell, she asked me if we would ever return to Moscow.

"I hope so—some day," I replied.

"But you are not sure?"

I wanted to be honest with her. "I can't be sure. Who knows in this world what's going to happen?"

"You will if you can?"

"Yes, Mama, I certainly will."

"Will you promise, both of you?" Her anxiety touched me deeply.

We promised. For the last ten years that promise haunted us both. Tamara had kept her part of the agreement almost upon our arrival on our return to Russia. Now, tonight, I would make good.

Under my arrangement with the Intourist bureau in London, I had paid for the use of a chauffeur-driven car three hours every day. As I prepared to leave the hotel for my mother-in-law's, I thought it was about time to begin using the automobile for which I was paying. With this in mind I called at the Intourist office on the ground floor of the National.

The office manager seemed to know who I was and with considerable exaggeration, she said, "Mr. Gilmore, as you speak Russian you will need no interpreter and as you know Moscow as well as we do, you will need no guide. Please, take the car whenever you want it and go where you like —within the regulations set out for foreigners."

"You are very kind. I shall need the car this evening."

"Here is the number of your car. Take it. Go where you like." This was indeed refreshing.

I directed the chauffeur to Ulitsa Krasina. I may not have known Moscow as well as the head of Intourist, but I certainly knew it better than this driver. But, with much giving of directions, I got him there.

Over the telephone Tamara's sister had told us that brother Vladimir, or Vovo, would be waiting for us on the sidewalk in front of No. 7, Ulitsa Krasina, to escort us to the apartment. I did not quite understand why this was necessary but, correctly attributing it to hospitality, I agreed.

Vovo was fifteen when we left Moscow. He was now twenty-five, married and the father of a two year-old son Aloysha. Dressed in a new fur hat and a dark overcoat, Vovo was immediately recognizable. I bounded out of the car and, knowing what was going to happen, braced myself. As long as I have lived in Russia I have never accustomed myself to being kissed on the mouth by men, dear to me though they may be. However—.

Arm in arm, we hurried up the three flights of stairs and there in the same apartment that I had first seen in the bitter winter of 1942–43, we had a real laughing, weeping, shouting, joyful reunion. All the women of my wife's family age slowly. In fact, they remain indecently youthful looking for their ages.

I am twenty years older than Tamara (and I look thirty years older), and, with embarrassing frequency, she is mistaken for my daughter. I feel certain that one of these days someone will identify her as my granddaughter and then I will be furious. As with Tamara, my mother-in-law holds back her years extremely well. Perhaps their Tartar blood, their high, tight cheekbones, and their luxurious brown hair that refuses to grey, have something to do with it, but I think a youthfulness of spirit is the answer. In any case, Tamara's mother looked to me exactly as she had a decade before, with her tall straight figure and her ageless hair.

Zina, my wife's elder sister, is the one exception to the ageless Chernashova women, but there are truly understandable reasons in her case. At the war's end, she married a young man in the Soviet Navy, a tall, handsome fellow with four wounds and an outstanding record in battle. I never set eyes on him for the obvious reason that if he had been discovered associating with me, or even meeting me, Stalin's henchmen would have suspected the worse. I had been shown many photographs of Alexei, however, and I felt I knew him. Two weeks after he married Zina, he was on his way back to his post as an adjutant to some admiral, when he was arrested and bundled into the Lubianka. It took his heartbroken wife eight months to confirm his arrest. Then it took another six months to learn that he had received a sentence of eight years on one of the most fantastic charges imaginable.

Alexei was accused of "lack of revolutionary vigilance," meaning that he, an officer of the Soviet Navy, had committed the crime of marrying a girl whose younger sister was the wife of an American correspondent. In the paranoidal atmosphere of suspicion that prevailed in Stalin's final years, Beria's policemen deduced that Alexei must have been spying for me. This, of course, left me with the shattering conclusion that they suspected me of espionage.

About this time, my two Russian secretaries were arrested. Knowing the pattern, I concluded that I would open *Pravda* or *Izvestia* one morning to read their denunciations of me, brought about under pressure, or worse. It never happened, but I have good reason to believe that after the plan had been decided upon, the political police changed their minds.

They certainly wanted to discredit The Associated Press —for one thing they have frequently claimed, quite preposterously, that this old and respected news agency is an arm of the United States government. After Stalin's death such nonsense was forgotten, but at the time of Alexei's arrest they clung to this view and I felt they were out to get me. Though it was not to be, William Oatis, the AP man in Czechoslovakia was arrested, and went to prison. It was not until after Stalin's demise and Beria's execution that he was released.

As for my brother-in-law, Alexei, with Stalin out of the way, his successors—to their eternal credit—released political prisoners by the thousands and Alexei was among them. He was told that in his case a terrible mistake had been made: he was not, and had not been, guilty of anything. He was repatriated from prison camp to his home in Moscow and given a written exoneration. The government was very sorry about what had happened—as indeed I am sure it was —but one thing was wrong. Alexei had lost his mind.

"They accused him of everything," an official told his wife, "and unlike so many others, he refused to confess." Of course, there was nothing to confess to, but in thousands of cases the wrongly accused, humiliated and tortured for days and nights, simply gave in and in their eagerness to halt the nightmare said they were guilty of the most heinous and improbable crimes. Not Alexei though. He stood up to them and in so doing his once fine mind gave away. That's why Zina looked as old as her mother.

Alexei could not be present for the reunion. "He's completely harmless, poor fellow," Zina explained, "but I must prepare him for meeting you, Eddy, and for seeing Tamara again. You see, the excitement might be too great for him."

I put my arm around her and kissed her.

"I'm afraid I'm slowly going blind," said Zina without the slightest self-pity, "but I live. I still work at the same old place. I've had a promotion or two and I think my superiors like and respect me, and the government has been fair and good to Alexei."

"Respect you," I broke in. "They should give you a medal."

"Not me. I've got Alexei back. That's all I want. That, of course, and for him to get well."

"Have the doctors tried?"

"The government has done everything. They've offered every help. We are still trying to help him, of course. But—," she smiled, "you and Tamara are back in Moscow and this is a special evening."

It certainly was, too. Vovo's wife, Nina, was a beautiful, small, dark-eyed, black-haired girl and their son, Aloysha, was one of those adorable round-faced Russian boys with unusual self-assurance. He put his tiny arms around my neck, kissed me and said, "Greetings, Uncle Eddy."

Tamara's mother, Natalia Afannasovna, and Zina and Nina had prepared a feast and it included—especially for me —a heaping plate of hot *blini*.

Apartment 137 had been completely re-decorated and

furnished anew, a living illustration of the better life now being enjoyed by the average Russian citizen. Instead of sharing it with her son and daughter, my mother-in-law now had it to herself. This is not strictly correct, for as Tamara explained to me, some relative from the country was usually in temporary residence. At this occasion, my wife's great-aunt, Marfusia, was stopping at Ulitsa Krasina.

I have experienced many surprises in the Soviet Union, but one of my biggest came on this reunion evening. Casually Tamara's mother turned to her and said, "Please dear, will you go into the kitchen, look in the refrigerator and take out the caviar?" Ten years ago this sweet and generous woman, in her wildest dreams, would not have imagined having the use of an electric refrigerator, much less owning one. Costly caviar would also have been out of the question.

My mother-in-law asked Vovo to make the first toast. Modesty prevents me from quoting it. When it was her time to sip and say something, she did not do the obvious. Instead, she raised her tiny glass of vodka and said very quietly and movingly:

"Our dear Eddy lost his mother but three months ago. We all remember when his father was killed during the war. It was just after he married our Tamara. Well, now my son Eddy has no close relative left, but I do hope that he knows that we are his family, that he is our close relative and that we love him dearly. No matter how much we love him, we could never replace a mother's love. I don't mean to say we could, but next to his dear departed mother's love, ours is the strongest."

It was a sentimental Russian evening, with the old samovar bubbling on the table before me, and with dear faces around the table, and I am afraid there were tears in my eyes.

At this moment little Aloysha, who had been playing with a new kitchen faucet attachment, as if it were a toy, smashed it.

"*Nitchevo*," said his father. "I was taking it home to

make a repair, but it doesn't matter. I'll get another one to-morrow."

This astounded me. In the Moscow of ten years ago, such a plumbing gem would have been so expensive and hard to come by that its destruction would have been a calamity. Now, it was laughed off as of minor concern.

As the evening wore on and the wine and vodka flowed in keeping with the conversation, Vovo asked me what I was doing wearing a Western felt hat in such Russian winter weather.

"I haven't been here long enough to buy a fur one," I said.

"You needn't bother. You shall have mine."

I told him I would do nothing of the sort. For one thing it was apparent that his had only recently been bought.

"Please accept it," said Tamara in English. "He will never understand if you don't."

"Then thank you," I said, "but you must take mine in exchange. A poor substitute I'll admit, but it's the best I can do at the moment."

When he placed his splendid new hat upon my head, it was a perfect fit. I repeated that he must take my hat.

"If you don't mind," said my brother-in-law, "I'd rather not."

"But I want you to have it."

"Do me a favor, don't force me to take it."

"Why not?"

"Excuse me," he said and I saw he was embarrassed. "Forgive me, but it's such a silly looking hat."

"All right, but you must take my tie."

"With the greatest of pleasure. I've been eyeing it all evening." I whipped it off and presented it to him.

Incidentally, while Tamara and I would have adored staying with her mother, it was simply out of the question. For one thing, the Soviets still employ the old block system. In every apartment house there is a house committee and every stranger spending the night in a Moscow apartment—where he or she is not a regular lodger—must register with the house committee. The registration of foreigners must be made with the police and foreigners may lodge in an apartment only with police permission. Before we left London, we were told that we had been assigned to the National—and that was that. Although we resided in the hotel, Tamara journeyed to her mother's apartment twice every day we were in the Soviet capital.

It was getting late and I knew it was time to go, but I felt I had to say something about Tamara, the girl I had taken to the West ten years before.

Putting my arm around her I said, "Since Tamara left Moscow she's been to many lands and met many people, some of them people in very high places. She's met Prime Ministers and Presidents and she's even been a guest of a Queen. I want you all to know that she's always carried herself with dignity and modesty and you should be proud of her."

"I'm very glad to hear this," said her mother, "but what sort of wife and mother has she been?"

"Wonderful in every way," said I.

"Then forget about the Queens and the palaces and the Presidents," smiled my mother-in-law. "If she's been a good wife and mother then we are proud." That put me in my place.

Since the establishment of diplomatic relations between the United States and the U.S.S.R. in 1933, the Moscow residence of American ambassadors has been Spaso House, the onetime home of a pre-revolutionary sugar merchant. Spaso comes from Spasopeskovskaya, the little square on which it stands. The present resident of Spaso House called us soon after our arrival and asked us to come out for an after-theatre supper, explaining that he and Mrs. Kohler had earlier booked seats for Pushkin's opera, *The Queen of Spades*, an arrangement which would be difficult to change.

We accepted with pleasure and planned on having a light dinner before going, but early on the afternoon of the supper, we received another call and were told that the ambassador had decided not to attend the opera and that he and the ambassadress would be pleased if we would come to dinner.

We were met at Spaso's large double door by one of two Chinese servants who have worked at the residence since that eminent foreign correspondent, Demaree Best, imported them with him years ago. Best left Moscow eventually, but the Chinese stayed on, serving a long line of American envoys extremely well. As we entered the ambassadorial Blue Room, we were not only greeted by the Kohlers, but by a loud shout from the far end of the chamber. The shouter was Ambassador Elbridge Durbrow, America's NATO envoy in Paris, and an old Moscow hand if there ever was one.

Durbrow is one of the brightest diplomats in the State Department as well as one of its most articulate. He has spent many years of service in Russia and knows the country and its people backwards, forwards and sideways. He is an advocate of the theory that a foreigner cannot build up good will with the Communist rulers, and to a fledgling correspondent who was having some trouble in understanding the Durbrow supposition, he put it this way: "They balance their books every night, and no matter how much you do for them, how pleasant you treat them, you'll start out in their eyes tomorrow morning being a son of a bitch all over again."

Greeting us in the Blue Room he said, "This afternoon when I thought we were going to the opera, someone said to me, 'Do you know the Gilmores are in town on a visit?' and I replied, 'Who in hell are the Gilmores?' When they told me, 'Tamara and Eddy,' I told them, 'To hell with *The Queen of Spades.*'"

It was pleasant to be told you were preferred to Pushkin and Tchaikovsky, but in all honesty it is a very lengthy opera and Ambassador Durbrow had probably seen it forty times.

Like Tamara and me, he was in Moscow on a short visit, and as we reminisced before a log fire I seemed to see before me all the men I had interviewed and talked to in this room, in these chairs, before this fireplace—Wendell Willkie, Joseph E. Davies, Patrick J. Hurley, General Dwight D. Eisenhower, Harry Hopkins, Eric A. Johnston, W. Averell Harriman, General Walter Bedell Smith, Admiral Alan G. Kirk, Alger Hiss, Edwin Stettinius, Cordell Hull, General George Marshall, James F. Byrnes . . .

In this room a high-ranking diplomat once confided to me that Stalin had agreed to enter the war against Japan. It was one of the most important secrets that I ever had to keep. It was also here and likewise off-the-record that I once heard a man—whose name is a household word in the United States and many other lands, a man known for his opposition to Communism—say in a burst of sudden Russian admiration, generated no doubt by excessive Slavic hospitality and a large amount of vodka: "Joe Stalin is a good fellow. I think America can do business with him. He impresses me as a man who will keep his word, and you boys, you newspapermen, if you write otherwise, well, I think you'll be doing a disservice to your country." Years later, he learned differently and I have often speculated what effect that statement would have had on his really phenomenal career, if he had been named as its author.

Mrs. Kohler, an elegantly dressed woman who has one of those small shapely figures made for clothes, or vice versa, asked us in for dinner. After a sumptuous spread, the Ambassador took Durbrow and me on a sentimental journey through Spaso House. Every room reminded me of something: the tall imitation marble column which a tipsy second secretary once tried to climb, only to end up on his back with a mild concussion; the ambassadorial private sitting-room on the second floor, where once hung a Soviet-made Great Seal of the United States (a Russian present), in which there was a not too cleverly concealed listening-device; the long gallery down which Harriman used to summon his private secretary by shouting, "Bob, oh, Bob" (Harriman told me that in choosing his secretaries he insisted that the young man be a former miler on his college track-team and that he also be a Phi Beta Kappa); the veranda on which Beetle Smith and Frank Roberts, now Sir Frank Roberts, Britain's Ambassador in Bonn, rehearsed every afternoon before their meetings with Stalin on lifting the Berlin blockade (William Barker, then first secretary in the British Embassy in Moscow, would assume the role of Stalin and his zeal to prepare Smith and Roberts for their East-West negotiations and the questions and proposals they might expect from Stalin, produced such knotty diplomatic issues that Smith once said, "Hell, Bill, you're worse than the old man in the Kremlin. You actually make me think harder," which was high tribute to Barker. After the lifting of the blockade had been negotiated, Smith told me, "Few people will ever know that young man's contribution to the Western cause"); the suite at one end of the building where, during a certain ambassador's absence from Moscow, one of his secretaries held a party that began on a Friday evening and did not finish until the following Monday morning at dawn.

Back in the Blue Room, Ambassador Kohler turned on the phonograph and we danced. Then someone put on a Russian gypsy record whose tempo was killingly fast. Durbrow, admitting he was fifty-nine, folded his arms and kicked his feet before him, performing a violent Cossack dance. It must have been about half-past one in the morning when the Spaso reunion party broke up and the occupant of Spaso thoughtfully sent us home in the ambassadorial automobile.

On the ride back to the hotel, I recalled that during one of the serious interludes of the evening everyone present agreed that vast changes had taken place in the life of Russia since Stalin's death. Earlier in his career, Kohler had been stationed in Moscow as minister-counsellor, and in discussing the differences since then, Mrs. Kohler had said, "It's so refreshing to be able at last to meet so many Russians and their wives."

In all of Russia, Moscow's Aragvai is one of the very few restaurants with real character. Its garish inelegance is so uniformly graceless, so consistently artless, that it endows it with a peculiar charm. Quentin Reynolds once said that the principal dining salon reminded him of the men's room at Grand Central Station. Being Georgian, the Aragvai is flamboyantly masculine with gaudy knife-wielding, muscle-flexing, maiden-saving frescoes from the saga, Twelve Nights in the Skin of a Tiger, adorning its walls. It has a number of private dining-rooms, also indelibly stamped with the decorator's meretricious motif. However, one does not go there to eat walls and the food can be superb. I have had some glorious parties at the Aragvai and entertained some very fancy and influential people, as well as some very beautiful ones. If you know the management and go to the trouble of explaining exactly what you want (as well as what you do not want), you are in for a fine evening of gastronomic enjoyment.

For me the Aragvai has sentimental associations, for the first time I met Tamara we dined there with friends, Dr. John Waldron, physician to the U.S. Lend-Lease Mission to Moscow, and the strikingly beautiful Russian girl he later married.

For years the restaurant's head waiter was Mikhail Stepanovich Malozemov, a man of short stature and great deportment. He wore his black hair long, and parted in the center it hung over his ears, framing his pale face like a pair of parentheses and making him look like Fydor Dostoievsky. In a proletarian nation he wore pince-nez on the high bridge of his nose, a starched collar and striped morning trousers with a tail coat, frayed and worn from years of service. In 1950, I believe it was, I bought him a new coat, braided and with a lining of silver figured silk. He wore it well and with pride and I was proud of him.

During our first week in Moscow we felt a pilgrimage to the Aragvai was in order. With a few friends we went there, but with no advance notice. The restaurant was still the same, except that my old friend was gone; died in harness, they said, and for all I knew, my harness. Well, bless him.

The assistant director (in Russia, restaurants have directors and often assistant directors) I recognized as a former member of the Aragvai orchestra, a broad-faced man with a shock of grey hair and large black-rimmed glasses. He seemed genuinely glad to see us.

"If you had only telephoned us, *gospodin*," he sighed. "Your old room is occupied, I'm afraid, and it would have given us great pleasure to serve you and your friends there again."

I told him any room would do—just so it was not the main dining salon with its ferocious decorations.

"Then please come this way."

He escorted us to a small room decorated in blue, gold and anemic pink. I knew this salon well, so well, in fact, that at one time I think I knew the location of its every listening device. In full view of the assistant director, I stood and wagged my finger before one small radiator grill.

"It's gone, *gospodin*," he laughed. "It really has." I thought he should have been embarrassed but if he was he did not show it.

"Never mind," I said, "you've probably got something better now to take its place."

"Oh, no. There's been a *bolshaia raznitza*. We don't have them any more."

I congratulated him on his promotion, to the directorship, for in my days as a regular patron I remembered him as the maestro of some sort of odd-shaped fiddle which he rested on his left knee and sawed with a strange bow gripped in his right hand. We gave him our order which included caviar, warm Georgian bread, *satsivi*, *shashlik* and, of course, vodka and Georgian wine.

As he prepared to leave the room he leaned over and whispered in my ear, "Everything as before, *gospodin?*"

"Of course," I replied, although I was not quite sure what he meant.

The food was as good if not better than in years past, though the service was highly energetic and at times almost acrobatic.

As we were digging into the *satsivi* (cold breast of turkey submerged in a cool sauce made with nuts) the assistant director appeared with the fiddle I remembered and three members of the band, one of whom greeted me as if I were some long-lost and favored *kulak* recently returned to earth. The rest of the players were strangers. Seating themselves in a corner, they played all of our old favorites and some new compositions. I liked particularly their Eastern version of "*Podmoskovnie Vechera*," which the British jazzman, Kenny Ball, made popular as "Midnight in Moscow."

The party grew in gaiety and a succession of Georgian and Armenian waiters appeared in the doorway asking, "*Mojno?* (May I?)" and when we replied, "*Mojno*," but giving the word a different inflection which made it, "You may," they would put down their trays and throw themselves into the solo dances of the Soviet South.

One waiter asked if he could sing. He had a fine tenor voice and sang the Georgian love song, *Seliku*, and then the comic number that best translates as "On a Corner in Yerevan."

At one point during the evening, Tamara and one of the girl guests, returning from the ladies room to our salon, saw on a coat rack the long grey uniform coat of a Colonel in the Moscow militia.

"What a beautiful coat and cap," Tamara commented to the Colonel who just happened (I hope) to emerge from his private dining-room.

"Would you like to try it on?" he asked.

Next a General stalked from the room and joined the discussion with a shout, "No, no, no. You must try mine. Come inside. It's hanging just there."

"Tomorrow night," laughed Tamara, blowing him a kiss and hurrying back to us.

I cannot remember when we left, but at the door we became involved in a round of reminiscences, first with the hat-check man and then with the old mustached doorman, both of whom I had known for nineteen or twenty years. Somehow we finally reached the snowy street and our cars.

"Come on back to my apartment—forgive me, your old apartment," said Preston Grover, outside. It seemed just the thing to do.

When I had left Moscow, the AP's office and my residence were in a wing of an apartment house on Ulitsa Narodnaya, a wing reserved for foreigners. Now (as then) twenty-four hours, day and night, a uniformed militiaman was on point duty before the front door of this block of flats. I looked into the face of the one I found saluting us, but he was no one I remembered.

"What's become of Uncle Mishka?" asked my wife.

"Uncle Mishka?" said the militiaman, "Why, we must have ten thousand militiamen named Uncle Mishka."

"Of course. I'm sorry. I remember Uncle Mishka from long ago. He was such a good friend with my children."

I stood there in the snowy night looking for the changes. For one thing, a children's playground had been constructed on a nearby plot of former waste land.

"Do you know this place?" asked the militiaman.

"This was our home ten years ago. Two of our children used to play around this door, with Uncle Mishka."

"A lot of changes have been made in ten years."

"Yes, I see."

"For one thing," he explained, pointing before us, "they've torn down the old Tagankaya Jail."

The jail and an open detention area used to stand at the

far end of our apartment house. I often thought its location showed lack of subtlety on the part of the authorities. What a way to remind foreign residents that there was a prison for miscreants, domestic or foreign.

"*Bolshaia raznitza* in ten years," said the uniformed man, using that expression again.

"I'm inclined to agree," I told him as we entered the building we knew so well.

Before the elevator sat a woman bundled to her eyes in a shawl. Opening her eyes, she stared in amazement and then jumped to her feet crying, "Tamara Adamovna, Tamara Adamovna, you've come back!"

She was a sort of nightwatchman-janitor, and she had been there before that elevator on our first night so many years ago at Ulitsa Narodnaya.

The reunion was warm and touching.

Upstairs in our old apartment there were many ghosts: the little foyer where I had my office; the square room beside it which belonged to Vicki and Susanna; the long corridor down which Susanna, at age two, used to scamper every morning to hop into my bed; the combination lavatory and wine closet; the living-room from which my beloved hand-printed wall paper had been removed; pieces of furniture that I bought in Stockholm; our old dining-room where one night I saw an American Air Force officer win more than ten thousand dollars in poker. It was like returning to your childhood home and finding everything so much smaller than you had imagined. I thought this odd, as I did not think it happened to adult memories.

Back again in the old apartment, where Tamara and I had to solve so many problems brought about by our marriage, I said to myself that I still had a problem. "Just as it was ten years ago," I mind-mumbled, "you've got to get her out again. Will there be difficulties? I wonder. I wonder."

7. After the Cossacks Burned Down the "Y"

Years earlier, when living and working in Moscow, I knew a mad Russian named Sergei Golubov. He was a bigger than life cloak-and-dagger type who could hardly tell you the time of day without looking over his shoulder to make sure that no one was listening.

Amusing and not unintelligent, he was a graduate of Moscow University who had done some post-graduate work in a small American college. While in the United States he became fascinated with the American idiom, and when speaking with me he insisted on using *his* kind of English. Aware that walls, floors and ceilings can hear—although God knows he never had anything of a secret nature to impart or ask—he had perfected an elaborate and irreverent vocabulary. Even in discussing a subject as innocuous as last week's football game, his behavior was conspiratorial. In commenting on international developments or local news, he was downright furtive, using the most elaborate off-beat names and figures of speech for prominent personalities, government departments, organizations and other matters of substance.

His word for politics was *asparagus*. The Kremlin was *Radio City*. He referred to ruling members of the Communist Party as *Cossacks*. When the Soviet Union's security apparatus was the People's Commisariat of Internal Affairs —or the N.K.V.D.—he referred to its headquarters, the Lubianka, as the *Y.M.C.A.* or "Y" for short. The American Ambassador was *Coca Cola*, capitalists were *cocoanuts*, Prime Minister Nehru of India was *Moonlight on the Ganges*, Foreign Minister V. M. Molotov *Stone Bottom*, Chiang Kai-shek *Shanker Jack*, Mao Tse-tung *Noodle Soup*, Dr. Adenauer *Buffalo Bill*, Stalin *Zeus*, President Eisenhower *Custard Pie*, the Moscow Arts Theatre *Madison Square Garden*, the Bolshoi Theatre was *Jockstrap Tech*, and pretty girls were *goats*. His list was long and I had forgotten most of it.

Even to one familiar with his key words, his erratic conversation was difficult to follow. For instance, on one occasion he took me between two parked cars on Moscow's Gorky Street and whispered, "I've met a new goat from Jockstrap Tech. Even a cocoanut like you would admire her. I'd like you to meet her, but she's afraid. Her daddy works in Radio City."

Sergei was tall and gaunt, with shoulders so high and square that he always looked as if he had on a pair of football shoulder pads beneath his loose jackets. His long spindly legs were lost in his floppy, bell-bottomed trousers, and when he walked he did not bend his knees, but swung his feet forward in arc-like strides that made him look as if he were walking on stilts.

I lost track of him about two years before I left Moscow. I had heard at the time he had been arrested and sent to a labor camp for associating with foreigners.

On the morning after our Aragvai dinner the telephone rang during breakfast.

"Good morning, White House," began a voice in English. I knew at once it was Golubov, because that was his name for me. "Welcome to Moscow," he went on.

"How did you know I was in town?"

"Ah, ha!"

After a lengthy conversation, which I only half-understood because I had forgotten so many of his code words, we agreed to meet later in the day in the coffee shop of the National.

Twelve years had changed him but slightly. He still appeared to wear shoulders pads and walk on stilts, but his furitiveness had disappeared. This made conversation easier as he was not forever glancing over his shoulder. We talked in generalities and then he asked, "Well, how do you like Moscow now?"

"Much better."

"It is much better. Santa Claus is a big improvement on Zeus."

"Who's Santa Claus?"

Nodding towards the Kremlin, through the window across Manezhnaya Square, he said, "The new man in charge of Radio City."

"Mr. Khrushchev?"

"Who else?" Wagging a spoon before me, he asked, "Tell me, what's the biggest change you've found?"

"Well, I've only been here a few days—"

"That's all right. It's long enough to tell. What is the biggest single difference in the Moscow as you knew it under Zeus and as it is now?"

"I think the terror has gone."

"Right." He cracked the table with his spoon. "And do you know why? I'll tell you, and it's one of the greatest changes to take place in Russia for years and years and years. After the Cossacks burned down the Y.M.C.A., everything changed for the better."

I whooped with laughter.

"Don't laugh. There's nothing funny about that."

"Certainly there isn't. I only laughed because you put it so—differently." And I repeated, "After the Cossacks burned down the 'Y,' everything changed for the better."

What he said was, of course, quite true. The Communist Party had at last put checks on the secret police. The Lubianka was no longer the most dreaded building in Russia, and the new leaders had subordinated the security organs to the Party. We were soon to receive many confirmations of this at first hand.

On the fourth day of our visit, as if by arrangement, the telephone in our hotel living-room began ringing. And it rang and rang and rang. The calls were from old friends, Russians we had not seen for years, because they had been too frightened to have contact with us during the last four or five years of our Moscow residence.

Some of the callers were the unfortunate ones who had disappeared in one or another of Stalin's purges, or waves of arrests, and had come back in broken health. The majority of those who telephoned invited us to their homes. The others we asked to the hotel, always ending the invitation with "providing, of course, that this will be all right." For the next few days we must have been entertained by, or played host to, a dozen old chums, from whom I received confirmation that the greatest single change in Russia was the disappearance of terror from the lives of the people.

"Nowadays when someone knocks on my apartment door at two o'clock in the morning," said an architect named Alexander A. Podkhutov, "I no longer automatically reach under my bed for my Siberian travelling clothes." With a wide golden smile he added, "Nowadays I know that the knock means not the secret police, but one of my neighbors who is a little tipsy and has lost his way home from a party."

Podkhutov knew the unspeakable terror intimately. Arrested in 1948, he spent eighteen months in the Lubianka before being moved to a camp above the Arctic Circle.

"I must apologize for my face," he explained, "but a human being's face will take only so much beating."

His face was lopsided, the right cheek too round and full and the left sagged badly, like a half collapsed basketball. His eyes were the opposite of being crossed; they stared from his tortured face in opposite directions.

The second old friend we saw was Maria A. Rakova, still tall, dark and shapely with eyes of a rare pale violet. She too had felt the icy arm of police terror. Maria was arrested in 1947 and, after ten days in the Lubianka, she realized she was going to have a baby, and this contributed to her black despair. One of her ordeals had been to be stripped of every shred of clothes and left naked with her fears in her cell. Even the bed clothes of her bunk had been removed. After several weeks of ceaseless interrogation—and worse—she confessed to all sorts of preposterous accusations. She was given a five year sentence.

Several of the unlucky Soviet citizens thrown into jail by Beria's men told stories of having to live naked in prison cells—into which guards and interrogators peered from time to time, and they agreed the humiliation of this did much to break their spirit.

As can be imagined, it had an especially demoralizing effect on women prisoners. "I would rather have been beaten," said Maria, "but they didn't beat me. Oh, they knew how to get at me all right." Her arrest had been in mid-winter and on her first night of incarceration, her clothes were taken from her and a unique horror added to her ordeal. Her all-male tormentors poured water into her concrete cell and shut off all heat. The water froze into a sheet of ice.

"I crawled on my bunk," she said, "and I got so cold that I actually welcomed the light glaring from an electric bulb hanging from the ceiling. Of course it revealed every wrinkle of my body, but somehow it made me feel as if my whole world hadn't turned into an icy nightmare."

She thought for a moment.

"I can't remember whom they thought I was spying for, the Americans or the British. I confessed, of course, and was sent to a labor camp."

Her beautiful face seemed to drain itself of all expression as she went on, "My baby was born in camp. She died. My poor husband—you remember him, don't you?—well, he received a sentence of twenty-five years and it was too much for him to bear. He managed to hang himself."

She shuddered, took a quick sip of wine and stared out through the hotel window at the Kremlin.

"No," said Maria. "We Russians aren't afraid of the big bad wolf any more because there isn't any big bad wolf."

She did not mention Khrushchev by name, for there was no need to do this. It was obvious that she was referring to him as she said in a flat voice, "I've got a good job now. I live in a nice room. All I want to do is to keep on living as I'm now living, and—" her voice was loaded with feeling as she turned once more to look at the Kremlin, "and—I hope *he* goes on living for another hundred years."

"Has he really made all that difference?" I asked.

"He has. I'd like to tell that to the world."

These two Russians, Maria Rakova and Alexander Podkhutov, and thousands upon thousands of others falsely jailed under Stalin, were liberated in waves after his death. I checked the story of this mass amnesty with many persons. Nearly all of them told the same tale. Only in minor details did they vary. The first to be freed were members of the Communist Party. Next came officers and soldiers of the armed forces, and then the great mass of ordinary citizens. They were returned to their home towns and, where they had families, were allowed to rejoin them. They were given priorities in getting jobs and finding housing. The government gave them money with which to buy clothes, some furniture and food enough to get them started in their new lives.

I would like to emphasize that not a single meeting I had with these reprieved men and women was arranged by the authorities. My wife was present at some of the meetings, but not all of them. There were no interpreters, guides or Intourist officials standing by or listening in, and my friends spoke freely. Every Russian I talked to agreed that the terror had vanished, but a few were apprehensive lest the swinging pendulum of the Party line sweep back some modern forms of repression.

"But if that should take place," said one of the sceptics, "I'm quite sure that things could never be as bad, anything like as bad, as they were in the Stalin days."

I asked him what he based this sort of reasoning on and the reply was, "If the Communist Party—of which I'm a member—is to receive the wholehearted respect and cooperation of all the Soviet people, it must for all time dissociate itself from terror. I think it has, and I don't think it'll ever return to them, yet—"

"Yet what?" I urged him to go on.

"I was going to say that there are repressions not associated with terror and the people don't want repressions either."

"Such as what?"

"Such as the denunciations of modern art. I should say abstract art, I suppose, and the criticism of some of our writers. We all know that no one's going to be put in jail for going against the Party line in art, or music, or writing, but if someone persists in opposing the Party, well, I feel very certain that he might find it difficult to earn a living."

I made no comment.

"I don't think you believe me."

"It's not that," I told him. "It's not that at all. It's that I'm astounded that you, a member of the Party, would make such statements to me, a foreigner and a foreign newspaperman at that."

"Yes, I have to admit this is a change. Of course we aren't seeing one another officially. We've known one another for a long time and I know you won't embarrass me."

"You mean you prefer that I don't quote you?"

"It's all right if you quote me because I think you're seriously interested in the changes taking place in our country, but I don't think you'd better quote me by name because I'm not sure that the changes have been all that great. We can complain, but I'm not sure we would be forgiven for criticising the system—yet."

"What do you mean by 'yet'?"

"I mean that someday we may reach the stage where criticism will not only be tolerated, but it will become a part of Soviet life."

"Do you really believe this?"

He smiled. "Not really, but it's a hope."

"You paid me the compliment of saying I was seriously interested in the changes. Thank you. I am interested in them. I also know that if your country and my country can't learn to live together, then it's not going to be much of a world."

"Then you believe in coexistence."

"In my interpretation of it."

"Hmm."

I repeated that one of the most pleasant surprises I had experienced was the experience of talking to a Soviet citizen and receiving the sort of answers I had received from him.

"I tell you," he said, "the changes have been greater than a lot of Westerners think."

Several Russians said they did not feel exactly free to meet foreigners whenever and wherever they liked. One woman, an English teacher, explained it this way, "The trouble is, no one has told us how far we can go and how far we can't go, and until someone tells me I'm going to be careful."

"But you are seeing Tamara and me."

"Eddy, we've known one another a long time. I love you and Tamara. I'm a Russian and I hope all the courage hasn't been pressed out of me. I just had to see you again."

"You mean this may be our only meeting?"

"I don't know. I'll have to think about it."

"I quite understand and we'll understand if you feel it's best not to have another meeting."

"Oh, come on," she said, "let's don't be so sad."

Another with whom I had a frank talk was the son of a famous actor. I had known him too in the period that I was commencing to call the old days.

"I bought an automobile three years ago," he told me. "It's been in the garage for the last two months." He shrugged his elegant shoulders. "No spare parts! What do they mean by selling me a car and then running out of spare parts?"

I asked if by "they" he meant the government.

"Of course not," he fairly shouted. "I'm talking about the bureau through whom I bought the car. The devils. I wouldn't hold the government or the Party responsible for a thing such as this."

"Excuse me," I interrupted, "but I don't follow your reasoning."

"Look here. The Party and the government made it possible for me to buy the car in the first place. It was the same Party and government that gave me my education, and gave me my job. It has been through them that I earn enough money to have a very nice apartment, and as you see, a servant and an automobile."

He was quite serious as he went on, "You can't expect the government and the Party to be responsible for spare parts for one man's automobile. They have delegated authority for such minor matters to others, others who've fallen down on the job. You watch and see, it will be the Party and the government who'll give hell to these slackers who don't make enough spare parts. But, to accuse the Party or the government, why, *gospodin* Gilmore, that would be nonsense."

This man was a Komsomol, meaning a member of the militant All Union Leninist Communist League of Youth, to give it its full name. Under Stalin, a conversation with a Komsomol in his own home in which he openly criticized anything in the Soviet Union would have been unthinkable.

At the twenty-second Congress of the Party in October, 1961, Khrushchev said: "Our carriage is now more erect, our breathing freer and our vision clearer." I was beginning to agree with him.

Another factor—and an important one, I think—has been in the relationship between the Communist Party leadership and the erring Party member. This factor is forgiveness. As someone has said, "When the Marxists wrote their textbook on human behavior, they included no chapters on innocence or forgiveness." So far as I know, they still have none on innocence. Approach them in innocence and you are likely to have a shock. Yet I found many cases of forgiveness.

8. Golden Girls
and Boys

It can be very disconcerting to have a pretty Russian girl look you smack in the eyes and say, "Come on, let's be decadent. I haven't been decadent for at least a week."

It happened one night just after our arrival, when we began circulating in the circle of Moscow friends.

Demanding to be taught the Twist (Margaretta pronounced it Tweest), she turned on the currently popular favorite, a hopped up version of "Mack the Knife," but unfortunately not the great one by Louis Armstrong. However, this record was sprightly enough for me.

It was a good party and I was the only foreigner present, unless Tamara be considered one. I was in the company of eighteen Soviet citizens. We danced, sang and talked until about 4:30 o'clock in the morning. Finally, on the way home a dozen of us tramped down the stairs of a new block of flats on the southern outskirts of Moscow, laughing and joking, and, I am afraid, making an awful lot of Russian-American noise.

As we reached the icy street, I instinctively looked up

and down the windy thoroughfare for the secret police car that ten years previously followed me wherever I went.

Reading my thoughts, an old friend, Pavel P. Orlov, a foreman in a tobacco factory slapped me on the back and said, "Eddy Eddyvich, nobody follows you anymore."

"No," I replied, "since I've been back I haven't spotted anyone and I'm an authority on cops from Soviet secret policemen to house dicks in Denver."

"I'm not sure I follow you. Especially when you use American slang."

"I said no one's been following me in Moscow. It's a delightful change."

"See here," he said, "things have changed a lot. Today, if you were being followed—which I seriously doubt—you wouldn't know it."

I smiled.

"This is 1963," said Pavel, "ten years after that *svoloch* Stalin died. We're more clever about such things, but I repeat, I don't think you're being followed. I don't want to hurt your feelings, but why do you think you should be followed?"

"That's something I've always asked too. For years I was followed though. They didn't even try to hide themselves. Four men in a little black car—three of Mr. Beria's men and a driver."

"Well, that's all over now."

"I wish I could be as sure about it as you."

The changes shaking Soviet society have excited the nation's youth into a golden dream of a free and unfettered future with lots of creature comforts.

The young man wants to lead a more private life, up to now a difficult thing in a land of vast collectivization and over-crowding.

He wants a comfortable modern apartment, and a shorter work week. The artistic ones want an opportunity to create beyond the narrow, but slowly widening, boundaries of the Party line. Some of the bolder ones want a satisfactory explanation of a system that could give birth to and allow the despotism of Stalin's twenty-five years of ruling the country—and assurances that such a nightmare will not happen again. The young woman wants more privacy in home life, to escape from having to live with her in-laws. She also wants better and cheaper clothes, food and cosmetics, abolition of night work, and relief from office and factory work so that she may devote her full time to making a home for her husband and her children.

Teen-agers like Margaretta want to be "decadent" every once in a while, without some prudish Komsomol blowing the ideological whistle on her. A great many of the Russians I talked to feel that Khrushchev has opened the gates that will, in time, cause a flood of change.

Valentina A. Ivanova, twenty-two and the mother of a three-year-old daughter, manages to work as a laboratory technician in a Moscow hospital and continue her studies towards a degree in medicine. She said, "Comrade Khrushchev has a splendid insight into, and understanding of, the problems of the younger generation. I don't know where he gets it. Probably from his very understanding wife and daughters (Mr. K has two daughters and a son). If all the decisions were left to him, we would have much greater changes. We know there are a few hardened conservatives in the Party who are trying to pull him back."

"How can you be sure of this?" I asked.

"That he's being held back?"

"Yes."

"I am sure. I could give you their names—"

"I wish you would."

"We're not that free yet," she said and added, "There are men in the Party who believe you must run the party the way Stalin did, and that if you don't, the country is going to drift into some sort of harmful bourgeois society. They think it has to be one way or the other."

A twenty-eight-year-old engineer, Sergei I. Morozov, said to me one evening, "Khrushchev and his associates have taken this country out of the long Russian winter. They are showing us the way to spring, but there's still a lot of sunshine to be let in."

Asked if he, like Valentina, felt that pressure was being put on Khrushchev to slow things down, he answered, "I don't completely share that view."

He frowned, thought for a moment and said, "Everyone —well, nearly everyone—has begun to taste the good young wine of life. It's very exciting because many of us have never tasted it before. We want more of it. We're going to get more of it, but I don't think we're going to be allowed to get drunk on it."

"Is it Mr. Khrushchev who's rationing the drinks?"

"He and his collective."

"Then you believe a collective leadership is directing affairs? You don't think Khrushchev has the full power of decision?"

"No. A collective is in command—I shouldn't say that. I should say in the big decisions Comrade Khrushchev's word is the law. You must not lose sight of the fact that he has men around him who think the same way he does. That's why there are no real disagreements on high. I don't think he would tolerate any real Stalinists in the Government."

"He allows Voroshilov to go on."

"Voroshilov is an old man and he has given his whole life to the Party and the country. Voroshilov is still respected. That's why he's tolerated. That's why Molotov and Kaganovich, why Malenkov and Bulganin are tolerated. They are harmless. They have no following."

"Then why does Malenkov live in disgrace and banishment?"

"He hasn't been disgraced. He does very useful work."

Having gotten this far with fairly ticklish subjects, I decided to bring up another.

"Since being back here," I told him, "I've heard many

strange stories about what's going on in this amazing land of yours. I've heard—and from a fairly good source too— that there are people on the Central Committee who think that there's a great deal in what the Chinese leaders in Peking are saying."

"I suppose you are going to say we've got Chinese in the Central Committee." He smiled. "You Western correspondents are always putting tags on things. You and your politicians are forever talking about how devious we Russians are. Sometimes your thinking is so devious that it's hard for us to follow it—especially when you think, talk and write about what's going on in the Soviet Union."

"But does this answer the question—are there members of the Central Committee who tend to side with Peking?"

"I'm not a member of the Central Committee, so I have no real way of knowing. But you forget, we have Party discipline. We follow the line laid down by the Party. I would seriously doubt if there are any followers of the Peking line in the Central Committee."

At her mother's home, I talked to a young and prominent actress. I will call her Galina.

"Life is fine," she said in answer to my leading question, "but what troubles some of us is the attitude of some people to the arts. When are we going to be allowed to do something new—I mean truly new—in the ballet, for instance? It's so old and stylized. I think the Bolshoi can be boring at times."

"The great Bolshoi ballet? Why, I know people in London and Paris who'd fight you for saying that."

"Agreed, agreed. You people who live in the capitalist countries, you are such defenders of—well, most things classical in Russia. But the Bolshoi is shockingly old-fashioned and some of their young people have lost spirit. They don't seem to want to try very hard any more."

"I don't know much about ballet, but I thought the Bolshoi was about the best in the world."

"I suppose it is, technically, but a lot of people in the Bolshoi don't think it's the greatest in the world. Do you know, they greatly admire the Royal Ballet in London. Many of them would give a great deal to work in London."

"You mean to run away as Rudolf Nureyev did? He's working with the Royal Ballet."

She frowned and said, after a moment of hesitation, "No, not like him. They don't want to work in London that badly."

I tried to pursue this subject, but Galina would say no more about it and remained silent when I asked questions.

"What about drama today?"

Galina brightened, as if relieved that I had dropped the subject of Nureyev.

"Yes," she began, "when are we going to do some new plays? I mean some really exciting plays. I don't know how much of the theatre you've seen since you've been back, but some terrible stuff is being put on as 'new.' I don't mind saying that some of it's awful. Now our films—things are better here. We have some young directors with marvelous ideas and they're putting them into their films."

The West is not alone in the jet age slackening of morals. A mother, whose late husband was a close friend of mine, told us, "I don't know what's become of morality in Moscow. I mean morality among the young. So many of our young people seem to have abandoned the standards of Russian and Soviet morality."

"It's the same back home—according to some people, especially in what's known as society."

"We have a sort of society here too, you know," she laughed.

"Don't tell me you have debutantes?"

"Of a sort, yes."

I should point out that this woman has lived in Washington and London.

"The society here that I'm talking about doesn't have the same base as yours, of course. The young people I'm talking about are the sons and daughters of high officials, military men, actors, singers and musicians, and some of them live rather wildly. Many of the girls don't bother to get married anymore. They just go off with some young man and they start living together."

"That's nothing new. People were doing that when I lived here. It was happening all the time."

"Not to the extent that it's happening now," she said, "especially among our Golden Ones."

"You still use that expression, I see."

"Yes. Is there a better one for the young people growing up in a Socialist state who have too many of the good things given them almost from birth?"

I asked what was the attitude of the Golden Ones towards children and family life.

"As you know, abortions were legal until, let's see, when was it? I believe it was in the early 1930's."

"I think it was 1936," I said.

"Thank you. Well, abortions were abolished, and then in 1956, they were once more legalized. As contraceptives are difficult to find and expensive, I'm afraid a lot of these girls go in for abortions. They just laugh about having them done and think nothing of it. And the parties that take place in some of the *dachas* around Moscow and down on the Black Sea coast in summer—oo, la, la."

I told her that what she was saying about morals and sex in the Soviet Union was all rather straightforward, and that while she might deplore it, I had the feeling it had been going on for a long time.

"Perhaps, perhaps, but there are other things less 'straightforward,' as you call them, that go on here and they worry a lot of mothers and fathers."

"May I ask you this," I said. "In this society, the society of the Golden Ones, are there homosexuals?"

"A few, but we don't make jokes about them. Pederasts are not amusing. I've never understood why you make jokes about them in the West."

"But you did say you have them, especially among the Golden Ones?"

"Too much importance shouldn't be attached to these people. Their number is insignificant."

This woman was the mother of two daughters, both pretty and popular, one eighteen and the other seventeen.

"About those parties you mentioned—"

"There are parties and there are orgies," she interrupted.

"Orgies in Moscow?"

"With degenerates, yes. Now because I'm talking to you frankly about these things, please don't get the impression that—well, that this sort of thing plays any important part in Soviet society. You journalists, you are all alike. Tell you something and you put too much emphasis on it."

"Surely this isn't the case with Soviet journalists?"

"I don't know many of them. I'm speaking of you Western journalists. I suppose you are going to write about things I'm telling you—"

"I would like you to say I may. I will not use your name, of course."

"Thank you. I'm trying to be helpful, but I don't want you writing something that will give the impression that Soviet society has no morals, that it's gone to pieces, or that a large number of our young men are pederasts. What I'm trying to say is that there is a breakdown in old-fashioned morality and I'm giving you some isolated examples."

"You are being most helpful. I can't imagine any sort of society without these things we are talking about. Since they are of interest to me, I imagine they would be to others."

"I'm glad we understand one another."

"You said something about orgies?"

She frowned. "It makes my neighborhood bad, but just

around the corner from here lives, or did live, a young man. His parents were decent, hard-working people and his father was a Party member. Well, one day this young man met one of the Golden Ones and that's when the trouble began. A few weeks ago the two young men were arrested. Not only had they been taking part in some of the finest old orgies since Rasputin's, they'd been organizing them."

"Organized orgies in Moscow, my, my."

"Two of our Golden Girls began sleeping with these young men and after a while one of the young men—I forget which one—got the idea of using the girls in a new sort of business. Private enterprise, you know. The girls said the young men threatened them and blackmailed them into what they did. Anyway, I'm afraid some shocking things used to take place around the corner, and the two young men began charging money to get into this apartment. The story got out and there were a number of arrests. Didn't you hear about it in London?"

"No, I can't say I did."

"The two organizers were arrested, tried and executed." I whistled.

"Tell me," I asked, "do you agree that the biggest change that has taken place in the Soviet Union since the death of Stalin has been the removal of terror from the lives of the people?"

"Yes, I suppose you could put it that way."

"But these two executions. Surely that's very severe punishment."

"Where is the sense of proportion you people from the West are always talking about? This was a very severe crime."

"What about the people who are being shot for speculation? It's very frightening."

"It doesn't frighten me."

"No? Do you really mean this?"

"It doesn't frighten me, because I will have nothing to do with speculators and I won't deal on the Black Market.

Neither will the great majority of people. Look here, Eddy Eddyvich, this is a socialist country. You can't have capitalism in a socialist country. The whole thing would go under if you did."

The Soviet Communists seem unable to make up their collective minds about crime and punishment. When the Bolsheviks achieved power in 1917, they decreed an end to the death penalty, but as civil war and the intervention of foreign armies threatened the life of the shaky young government, its desperate and fumbling leaders reinstituted capital punishment. At first they limited it to the crimes of counterrevolution, speculation and banditry, only to learn that there was no cure-all or panacea for the numerous social illnesses plaguing the new state. So death by shooting was extended to cover a long list of offenses.

Six men were executed for assaulting a girl. Four years later, four persons lost their lives for hoarding silver coins that should have been turned in to the state bank. Those were desperate days, of course. Collectivization was widely unpopular and, in resisting it, many peasants and workers committed arson and sabotage on the farms and in the factories. More Soviet citizens paid the supreme penalty. A group of railway workers were shot for negligence, alleged to have been responsible for a train wreck that killed seventy people. Soon the death sentence was pronounced on thieves and pillagers.

In the U.S.S.R., of course, much belongs to the State. Steal a cross-tie from a branch railway line in some forlorn district of Siberia and you have pilfered the property of the Nation. As Stalin succeeded Lenin, he determined to crush all resistance to the revolution and ordered that capital punishment be handed down for a variety of law violations, saying: "The thief stealing the property of the public is as bad as the spy or the traitor, if not worse. He who steals from the Commonwealth, steals from all."

High Party officials continued to proclaim that redemption of the criminals was their principal concern, yet the number of executions and deportations to Siberia mounted. Seeking to justify the increasing list of shootings, Commissar of Justice Krylenko said:

"This punishment is applied to those who offer no hope of reform, to the class enemies whose whole activity has been directed against the Revolution, or to those who have broken with society to such a point that it is impossible to adjust them to it. But according to our law, the death penalty is a temporary measure against the gravest of crimes; against those who menace the very basis of the proletarian state; and it is applied only as a measure of exceptional defense pending its complete abolition."

Following the end of World War II, the authorities did announce the abolition of the death sentence. Then, when the sub-zero political weather of the Cold War gripped the country, it was clamped back on once more. Stalin died in early March, 1953 and as political prisoners were released by the hundreds of thousands (some say millions), executions dropped off to nothing. From then until mid-1961, only first degree murder, sabotage and armed banditry were capital crimes.

In the relative liberty of the early post-Stalin years, swindling, black-marketeering and numerous rackets—some as complex as the Russian character—became a menace to society. Stalin's successors moved to crush it, and again the death penalty was dealt out to those found guilty of large-scale economic offenses, forgery, and violence in prison by hardened criminals.

Two and a half months later violations of currency regulations was added to the list of crimes punishable by death. In December, 1961, bribery, rape and assaults on militiamen became crimes for which citizens could be shot.

There was revulsion in the West as two men were executed for selling apples and making a profit on them. They had been caught peddling inferior apples and charging the price set for first grade apples only. Another man was arrested because he possessed several thousand American dollars. His accusers said he had bought them from tourists, as indeed he probably had; this was against the law and he lost his life.

A Muscovite converted his none-too-large apartment into a sort of night club and made a staggering rouble profit by additionally turning it into a place of assignations. As I have said before, Soviet girls are fairly free with their favors—to the men they love—but one of the big problems of many a young couple in love is where to go to make love.

During the warm Russian summers, Moscow's big Park of Rest and Culture is a favorite place, for all of its acreage is not devoted to resting and cultural activities. Away from the center of things, there are inviting patches of grass, clumps of bushes and a number of secluded spinneys. In winter, of course, the park is out; even the most ardent lovers could hardly keep their passion aflame in the cruel snows and sub-zero winds that whip across the Great Muscovy Plain. As few young men own automobiles, back seat romancing in a lover's lane seldom takes place. There is no hope of walking into a hotel in the Soviet capital and renting a room for a few hours. So, one can appreciate the fact that offering an apartment with warm beds, recorded music and soft lights—or no lights—could become a highly profitable business, and hence a violation of the laws of the socialist state. Alas, the embryo night-club, assignation-house amateur operator was unmasked, arrested, tried and shot.

Within the last twenty-nine months, more than one hundred persons have been sentenced to death for economic crimes, some of them involving the sort of transaction that in some Western countries would be looked upon as nothing more than making a fast dollar, pound, franc or mark.

Half way through 1963, the number of published death sentences for economic crimes totalled fifty-one. These shootings created no indignation, resentment or serious regret among the people with whom I discussed the issue of capital punishment in the U.S.S.R. After one shooting for what seemed to be a fairly mild misdemeanor, a Russian told a British newsman, "It's better than under Stalin. At least they shoot the *right* people now."

Another said, "These (the executed) are not real men. They are apes left over from a bygone age. They have no right to live in our society. What else could you do but shoot them?"

I was in the company of several Russians—men and women —one evening when someone related how a trio of Ukrainians had been executed for making a private profit on hair ribbon.

"It's the principle of the thing," said a young railway official. "It's just as bad as if they'd sold five hundred kilometers (312 miles) of ribbon. The ribbon belonged to the State, which means the people, and they were stealing from two hundred twenty million Soviet citizens. But," he warned turning to me, "please don't go thinking and writing that this means the terror is still with us. That would be wrong. It's harsh punishment, all right, but it must not be confused with terror. We have no more of that."

9. Beria, the Georgian Bedbug

If Moscow has a haunted house, then it is the home of the late Lavrenty P. Beria. The best known of his several titles was probably that of chief of the People's Commissariat of Internal Affairs (N.K.V.D.), Stalin's dreaded secret police. Standing behind a wall, just off the broad Sadovo-Kudrinskaya, a few hundred yards south of the house where the writer Anton P. Chekhov lived for a number of years, it is a squat, inconspicuous dwelling bordered on two sides by a bit of garden, with a front door that opens on to a sidewalk.

I am not sure how long Beria made it his home, but as early as 1942 it was pointed out as his abode in the capital. The report was that he, unlike most of the members of the ruling clique, maintained no *dacha* outside Moscow. Several times during and after the war, when visiting friends on nearby Granatnyi Perelouk, I saw Beria in front of his house, either in the act of entering it from his automobile, or leaving the place for his waiting car. Each time he was accompanied by a phalanx of bodyguards.

Beria was an odd bird. A Georgian, like Stalin, he did not greatly resemble his fellow countrymen who tend to be dark, noisy and aggressively masculine. Hirsute as bears, they wear mustaches and sideburns as if they were part of their national costume. Beria was clean shaven, and the pince-nez he wore gave him a pedantic, bland look which, as I understand it, was hardly in keeping with his character. A womanizer, he was forever afraid that he would contract a venereal disease.

I once knew a Russian whose father was a prominent Moscow physician. On one occasion, about two in the morning—the time of the day chosen by the N.K.V.D. for making their swoops—the doctor was awakened by a knock on the door of his apartment. Fearing the worst, he opened up and sure enough, there stood the unmistakable representatives of the secret police. Icily polite but uncommunicative, they simply directed the terrorized man to dress and take his medical bag with him. Saying a tearful farewell to his shocked family, he was bundled off down the steps of his apartment house and into a waiting automobile—only to reappear at his home within the hour.

"It's mad," grumbled the outraged but relieved physician. "Completely mad." He related how he had been hurried to Beria's house where he found the frightened commissar convinced that he had contracted gonorrhea, or worse, on a flying visit to Berlin.

It was no hastily awakened medical man who arrived at Beria's house on that day in the summer of 1953, however. It was a squadron of tanks, their guns loaded and ready for action. This startling event took place during that turbulent period of uncertainty immediately after Stalin's death; the tanks and their commander had come to fetch the head of the secret police.

Since then, Soviet leaders have told several versions of Beria's actual arrest and execution. Yet scores of Soviet citizens, and a few Americans from the nearby United States Embassy, remember the squadron of tanks and the wild rumors that followed their appearance at Beria's home. After his arrest and the subsequent announcement that he had been tried and found guilty and executed for treason and conspiracy, his home remained vacant for several months.

Then—and this is so very Russian—it was converted into a kindergarten. But it did not remain a kindergarten for very long. The Russians are a deeply superstitious lot. Many believe in ghosts and the existence of evil spirits and evil places. A woman who lived and still lives in the neighborhood told me, "My little boy was there for a while. He became nervous and frightened as did many of the other children. I took him away. The place was haunted." I talked to another mother whose child attended the kindergarten on Sodovo-Kudrinskaya. "My little girl couldn't bear the place," she said. "Games were no fun there and during the rest periods she was unable to sleep. She begged me to remove her."

Other Russians I talked to, however, scoffed at the idea that the house was haunted. Yet most of them, when I pressed them, admitted they would not like to live there, even if it meant the luxury of real living space and a bedroom for every member of the family. These scoffers, I should point out, were in a minority.

The majority of the Muscovites with whom I discussed the Beria house were convinced that it is haunted, insisting that strange things go on there at night. Two or three insisted they had seen unexplained lights hovering over the roof on dark evenings.

"Black cats meet there," volunteered an old woman named Lydia Mikhailovna, whose last name I know not. I met her at the apartment of mutual friends and she made a vivid impression. "It's a meeting place of dark spirits. What better place could they find. It's an evil, evil house."

"Lydia Mikhailovna knows," said my host. "Tell him your story, Lydia Mikhailovna."

In silhouette, she resembled an out-sized fire plug. Her head was completely round, like a small, ripe honeydew mellon, and perched atop her short neck and sloping rounded shoulders, it was like the nut adorning every fire hydrant's dome. From her shoulders to the ground, her long, shapeless, un-belted dress hung in a straight line. Being exactly the same size at the chest as at the waist and hips, her vital statistics probably would have worked out as, say, 42–42–42.

In keeping with many Russian women of peasant stock, she was mulishly stubborn and independent. In all of Russia, the Lydia Mikhailovnas, as a type, seemed less afraid and intimidated by the henchmen of Stalin and Beria than any other group I ever knew. On dozens of occasions I have seen these resolute old women defy authority and get away with it. Eking out their existence on pensions, and usually sharing a room with someone else, they were, in Stalin's time and now, generally allowed to go their defiant way.

In 1952, about a year before Stalin's death, Lydia Mikhailovna was suddenly ordered to vacate the room she shared with another *bobushka*. It was located on the fifth floor of a brick and mortar building fifty yards from the Arbat, one of Moscow's main thoroughfares. Someone with a higher priority than this pair of old ladies (it would not have had to be very high, for theirs was just about at the bottom of the social scale) wanted their room and there was nothing for them to do but move. They complained bitterly, but it got them nowhere. They were directed to shift their meagre furniture and belongings to an apartment house which just happened to be located almost directly across the street from Beria's house.

Still protesting, Lydia Mikhailovna and her companion made the move, but they insisted to the high Moscovy heavens that this was no way to treat two senior citizens, both of whom had refused to panic and evacuate the capital in 1941 when the Germans all but reached the city. They had, in fact, been given the Defense of Moscow medal.

Living across the road from Beria affected Lydia Mikhailovna in an odd and personal way.

She did the daily shopping for herself and her friend and, as she patronized a nearby peasant market, she found that the best and quickest route to and from the market, included about seventy-five or a hundred yards of Beria's sidewalk. She could have altered her way to the market, of course, but in her stubborn manner she insisted that by following the wall around Beria's house, she was shielded from the wind in winter and during the summers it was the shady side of the street.

"Besides," she added, "they always keep his sidewalk swept clean of snow and ice and they sand it regularly."

Her insistence on taking this chosen route to the market would have presented no problem, had it not been for the uniformed and plainclothes policemen who, twenty-four hours of the day and night, patrolled the sidewalk outside their chief's dwelling. As Lydia Mikhailovna's hours of marketing often coincided with the time of Beria's comings and goings, she was constantly being shooed away by loud and discourteous shouts of, "Hey, you, *bobushka*, you clear off, he is coming. Get away. Can't you hear?"

As she never altered her gait—no matter how much they yelled at her—she was forever being shouldered and pushed to the middle of the road or the other side of the street. As one chasing followed another, her exasperation mounted.

One morning when the thermometer showed about eighteen degrees below zero and the old woman was particularly fed-up with the regimentations of Soviet life, she was making her way along the sidewalk when she sighted the long black car of Comrade Beria purring up the street towards her. She lowered her head, but did not break her gait and as she neared the official's door the big chauffeur-driven Zis swerved into the sidewalk and stopped.

"Hey, you, *bobushka*," shouted one of the goons behind her, "Stop, stop, stop!"

The old woman plunged on.

Three uniformed men and several in plainclothes rushed her at the very moment Beria stepped from his automobile.

For a terrible moment, Lydia Mikhailovna, the chief of the secret police, and his shouting bodyguards, merged.

Strong hands tore at her coat, but Lydia Mikhailovna, now thoroughly enraged by the shouts, the manhandling, and her close proximity to the second most feared man in Russia, wriggled from their grasp and righted herself in time to address the startled Beria as follows:

"You great Georgian bedbug—"

At that one of the bodyguards slapped her across one ear, while another clawed at her throat. Aghast, Beria froze and his Adam's apple bobbed up and down as he gasped in astonishment.

"Bedbug," gasped Lydia Mikhailovna, "who has bloated himself"—another slap—"on the blood of the Russian people!"

A fist crashed against her head and the old woman rolled on the sidewalk at Beria's feet.

Dazed by this audacity, Beria threw up his right arm as if to shield himself from a blow, and staggered through the front door of his house.

Lydia Mikhailovna had, of course, gone far too far this time. She was picked from the sidewalk and removed to a nearby militia station. After sharp questioning by top echelon security officers, she was tried and sentenced to three years in a labor camp—at the age of seventy-two.

She served but thirteen months of her sentence, for her release quickly followed Stalin's death and Beria's execution. She was not only absolved of all charges, but was actually re-assigned to her original room off the Arbat.

Now eighty-three, she was remarkably alert and sharp of tongue.

"Why'd you call him a bedbug?" I asked her.

"A *Georgian* bedbug," she corrected me. "A Georgian bedbug who'd fattened himself on the Russian people's blood."

Today, Beria's old house is the Tunisian Embassy. The present envoy is reported by his diplomatic colleagues as saying that, as far as he is concerned, it is only another house.

"But that's not the way it was with the wife of his predecessor," explained one of her friends, the wife of a Western ambassador with whom I had lunch. "She told me she was frightened to death of the place. She said all sorts of strange noises kept her awake."

"You actually talked to her about the house?" I asked my hostess.

"Of course I did, and more than once too. She complained that at night the house was full of groans and unexplained footfalls and the slamming and banging of doors."

"What about black cats and lights hovering over the roof? Did she say anything about them?"

"No," laughed the ambassadress, "I'm afraid not, but I think it finishes off Lydia Mikhailovna's story very nicely."

Finding your first hidden mike in Moscow is a bit like having your first baby. Each is an advent of considerable importance, one that can have a direct bearing on your entire future. In a way, both microphone and infant intrude upon your home life, causing you and your wife to tip-toe around and speak in lowered voices, and they emphasize the seriousness of one's existence and its many pitfalls and responsibilities.

During my residence in the Soviet Union I heard at first hand many accounts of foreigners discovering listening devices that had been planted in their flats and offices, and I was once present in the map room of a Western Military Mission when a middle-aged and super-suspicious Colonel located six iron ears concealed behind six metal ventilators. I also saw for myself how a trio of live microphones had been planted in a room used by the personal staff of a British Foreign Secretary during a post-war conference in Moscow.

It was not I, however, who actually found the listening

device in my apartment in the Soviet capital, but a young electrician from the American Embassy. It was black, squat and ugly, with a glittering magnetized center that glared at me like an evil eye. As he detected it and, after some deft carpentry, lifted it from the wall between my bedroom and living-room, I felt a peculiar horror and experienced a sensation of violation that is difficult to express. In a lesser degree, I had the same feeling on returning to my home in America one night and finding that it had been entered and burglarized.

Over the twelve years I lived in Russia, I dwelt in a number of places, in hotel rooms and suites, apartments, a *dacha*, and a small house. It was at my last place of residence, an apartment on Ulitsa Narodnaya, that the microphone was un-walled. So far as I know, it was the only listening device I ever lived with. Yet how can I know for certain?

Moving into the new apartment, after it had been reconditioned and redecorated by the Soviet Government agency that theoretically served the foreign Diplomatic Corps and foreign correspondents, I was advised by an American friend to have the place "bugged"—as he put it. Bugging meant having it searched for listening devices.

Armed with what appeared to be a sort of gadget with which mines are detected on battlefields, the electrician began a careful check of every room. As we started in the living room, he did not have to look very long.

"If there's anything electrical, or even metal, in the walls," whispered the young technician, "it's going to show up here."

He pointed to a meter that appeared to be a snowshoe mounted on a vacuum-cleaner handle. The east wall registered nothing on his meter. Neither did the north and south walls, but when he reached the partition separating the living-room and the principal bedroom, at a spot about hip high, he stopped his sweeping motion and put one finger to his lips. Then he nodded to the meter. Its single white hand had swung from the left to far right. Slowly he moved the snowshoe contraption away from the spot, and the white hand swung back to a resting position. Now back to the suspect spot on the wall and once more the meter hand plopped over to the right.

Carefully, very carefully, he rested the contraption on the floor, took a notebook from his pocket, scribbled something and showed me what he had written.

"That's where your dog is buried," said the message. "Want me to dig him up?"

I nodded.

I will not go into all details, but he neatly removed part of a sheet of wall paper, carefully cut into the plaster and lathes and pointed to a black metal object about the size of a small saucer. Working with care and precision, as I imagine safe-crackers do, he at last removed the gadget, freeing it from a set of wires that vividly made me think of a small octopus being separated from its tentacles. From his work box he took a square metal object with contact points, placed it where the listening device had been and fastened the wires to the points. He plugged up the hole with something that looked like a square of black tile, and over this, meticulously affixed the wall paper. It was a thoroughly efficient job and would have taken a very practiced eye to discover any tampering with my wall.

"Let's go back to my office," he said.

At his office in the Embassy, we had a long and technical discussion about listening devices.

"The one they had in your place," he said, "was a pretty clumsy job. There's a lot about it I don't understand—why, for instance, they put it between two walls. This thing's not sensitive enough to pick up much, even if they suspended it from your ceiling like a chandelier. But sunk in the wall that way, you'd have to shout pretty loud for that thing to pick it up. Nope, I just don't get it."

"Well, I suppose they figured they were dealing with a pretty crude fellow."

"This could be—" he said and then he stopped himself.

"Could I come back next week and go over the rest of the apartment? I really should have done it today, but I got a little excited, and I wanted to show you the thing and talk about it."

The discovery of the listening device and my talk with the young electrician took place in 1952, and now my wife and I were going back to our old apartment during the first week of our return visit to Moscow. The occasion was a cocktail party, given for us by its present occupant. The living-room was loud with voices as we entered for, as with most cocktail parties in any part of the world, too many people had been packed into one room. I saw some familiar faces and met a great many new ones. Glass in hand, I somehow felt drawn to the wall where the microphone had been discovered and felt a strong urge to tell the story of what the electrician removed from that wall eleven years before.

Two ambassadors were my audience and as I finished my account, I asked, "Do they still plant those things?"

This was met by silence, an embarrassed silence, I thought.

"Ah, well," I said, "I guess times have changed."

"So have the listening devices," said one of the envoys, dropping his voice to a whisper.

"You mean they're better today?"

"These are vintage years," he replied.

"How so?"

"Why, I hear the Russians have perfected things to the point that they no longer have to plant devices in a room. With the use of new techniques, they can boom a sort of sound beam or ray in on you, through walls, through houses, from a distance of several hundred yards. You know, beam it right into this room and focus on a point—say, right here." He held a forefinger between his face and mine.

"Very interesting," I told him.

"See here, Gilmore, you've lived in this country long enough for me not to have to tell you that, no matter how many changes you notice in the Russia of today, you should still be very, very careful."

"Thank you, Mr. Ambassador."

"I hope," he said, "I haven't sounded too melodramatic, but I felt I should warn you."

He smiled and patting me on the shoulder said, "Let's change the subject."

After a bit of chit chat he and the other ambassador moved off, but the wife of one of the men remained by my side.

"Mr. Gilmore," she said very quietly, "there's something I'd like to tell you. I think your wife's a very brave girl."

"Brave? In what way, ma'am?"

"In coming back here. Coming back to Russia."

I felt a chill at the back of my neck.

10. "Pley Ett
Kule, Man"

After the ambassadress chilled me with her well-meaning but ominous observation on my wife's bravery in returning to Russia, I felt that a hot dinner was in order. Tamara agreed.

"The National or the Aragvai?" she asked.

"Neither, if you don't mind," I said. "I've had a youth café recommended, a place where I'm told you can hear good jazz and get a fair meal. Willing?"

"Off korse, Hoaney."

With a heavy tip and a broad foreign accent, I got us in and succeeded in securing a table to ourselves, no mean accomplishment in any Moscow eating place at 10:30 o'clock in the evening. The food was fair, but instead of traditional jazz, the Dixieland brand I like so well, we were greeted with some stuff as far out as Dave Brubeck.

"Cool jazz in Russia,'" I muttered, "who'd thought it?"

"What's kule djhazz?" asked Tamara.

"The stuff you're listening to right now. Do you like it?"

"It's all right," she replied, "but it's more fun looking at the girls." She nodded towards one Moscow miss dancing cheek-to-cheek with a young man with an open-necked sports shirt.

She wore green mascara and long false lashes.

"All right," I said, "you watch the girls while I try to figure out this music."

"You mean you'll try to figure out the music while also watching the girls."

"Have it your way."

"No, that's your way."

As we had arrived late, the band played only three or four sets before it was midnight and closing time. The leader was the last man to leave the stand, and as he passed our table, I said, "Interesting music, but when did cool jazz reach Moscow?"

He smiled, kissed Tamara's hand and, surprisingly, asked if he might sit down.

"Please do, and what will you have to drink?"

"Cognac, please."

In Moscow you do not have to order doubles, or large drinks. A single shot is a staggering slug. As the young musician knocked his back without so much as a blink, I ordered two more drinks for him.

"About cool jazz," I began, "is it really popular here?"

"A great many musicians would like to play it, but they're nervous about playing it. You see, they frown on kule djhazz as much as on abstract art."

"Really?"

"Oh, yes."

"Yet you still play it?"

"They," he said, "don't come in here."

He did not have to explain whom he meant by "they," but I could not resist asking.

He gulped another drink of raw cognac before replying, "If you know enough to question me about kule djhazz, then you know who I'm talking about." That modulated me.

"Excuse me," I confessed, "of course I know whom you mean. I shouldn't have asked you."

"*Nitchevo.*"

"They may not come in here, but it seems to me that news of, well, your sort of abstract musical tastes might get back to them."

"Well, *gospodin*, I doubt if they have the faintest idea of what I'm playing. And, if they ever asked me, I'll tell them that it's a djhazz improvisation on Prokofiev. Prokofiev is now perfectly respectable, and as they're always urging us to play Russian music for dancing, I'll tell them that that's exactly what I'm doing—and no one will be any the wiser. But, as I say, they won't know what I'm playing. I'm safe."

He hesitated before asking if I were an Englishman.

"My wife and I live and work in England, but I'm an American."

"You Americans don't have it all your way with kule djhazz anymore. Dafe Brrhubach is good, but the Czechs are playing revolutionary djhazz. It's very, very kule. And the Bulgarians are coming along too."

I asked if he had heard Benny Goodman when he made his trip to the U.S.S.R.

"Oh, yes," he replied with a slight frown.

"What's the matter with Goodman? I remember when a Benny Goodman record used to bring a hundred roubles in Moscow."

"We admired Goodman's tone and his execution, but if you'll pardon me, he's too old-fashioned for most Russian musicians."

"The public loved him, didn't it?"

"What does the public know?"

"You mean you really didn't like Goodman. You astound me."

"Sorry," he smiled. "Too, too old-fashioned. We've grown beyond that stuff."

"This," I said, changing the subject, "is an unusual place."

"There are several like it in Moscow. I even know of two or three in Siberia."

"Cool jazz in Siberia."

"Yes. Kule djhazz in Novosibirsk."

"Might make a good name for a tune. You say there are other places like this in Moscow. Are they as popular as this one?"

"I think we play more of it here. You came in late, didn't you?"

"Yes."

"Well, earlier we had some poetry reading. We played kule djhazz in the background."

"My wife and I must come back and hear it. What sort of poetry?"

"Modern, Soviet poetry. Some of our young poets are wonderful."

"Who are the best?"

"Andrei Voznesensky, Bulat Okudzhava, and of course, Evgeny Evtushenko."

"He's your Angry Young Man, isn't he?"

"I don't understand."

"It's a Western expression. But tell me, what sort of music do you play to the poems?"

"I told you—kule djhazz."

"Yes, but what compositions? What tunes?"

"Well, Voznesensky goes well with *How High the Moon*."

"I must listen to that some day."

"Do that, and then you can go back to America and tell them about it and perhaps they'll will start having poetry readings to kule djhazz."

"In America, I think they've read poetry to just about everything. Perhaps even to *How High the Moon*. That's an American tune, you know."

"I know."

"Suppose they walked in and heard you playing *How*

High the Moon. I don't care how you play it, I don't think
you can make it sound like Prokofiev."

"No," he laughed, sinking his final glass of cognac. "If
they asked me what *How High the Moon* was, I'd tell them
it's one of my improvisations on Shostakovich—"

He glanced over his shoulder before he said, "And they
don't know any more about him than they do about Prokofiev."

He stood up and shook hands.

"Don't laugh," he said, "but I shall speak English."

"We won't laugh."

"Pley ett kule, man," he said. "Pley ett kule."

Moscow's foreign diplomatic corps—which in Russian is
not called a corps but a corpus, a linguistic factor that over
the years has led to disparaging comment—is made up of
hard-working, serious-minded, intelligent, patient but long-
suffering and frustated men and women. The great majority
of the corpus is genuinely interested in the Soviet Union and
friendly disposed towards its citizens with whom they have
limited contact.

Under the present Soviet regime, life is easier for the
foreigner in Moscow than it has been for many years, but it
is not perfect. Ideally, I suppose, the diplomat in a foreign
country should have easy access to members of the government and its legislative bodies along with members of the
general public. But with the Cold War, which all but adds
up to an awkward armed truce between East and West, the
foreigner in the U.S.S.R. lives a restricted life. Yet, it varies
from embassy to embassy, and within the various embassies.
The difficulty of communication is enormous; while most of
the foreigners stationed in the Soviet capital read Russian,
many speak it and understand it badly.

Shopping is a nightmare for many Western women, and
back in Moscow this was a complaint I now heard again and

again. For one thing, in many Russian stores the customer is treated with indifference bordering on open hostility. The across-counter exchanges between shopper and saleswoman often sound as if the two were about to square off for violent combat. This is even more applicable to the Russian shopper and the counter-keeper than to the foreign woman, because in her own language the Soviet citizen is obviously more articulate. The attitude of the person behind the counter is that she is doing an extreme favor to the shopper in allowing her to remove a precious consumer item —no matter the cost (and the cost, by Western standards, is often staggeringly high).

I understand the attitude of the Russian saleswoman, but I do not like it. A contributing factor to the abnormal shopping situation is the fatalism and passivity of the Russian people, which has led to their putting up with all sorts of outrages against the individual. And then there is the Bureaucrat. This bumbling, fumbling, pompous, maddening individual has for a century and a half provided the Russian writer with a rich and realistic theme. In his wisdom, Lenin once said, "Russia is now a Soviet state disfigured by bureaucracy."

Zavtra (tomorrow) is for thousands of Russians the most ideal time, and the habit of never doing today what can be put off until tomorrow is ingrown in the Slavic soul. Progress, however, is being made.

Soon after our arrival I met an American mother of four children. From what I could tell, she was a sweet and sensible person from an upper middle-class professional family. She asked me how I found things after being away for ten years and, when I told her they were greatly changed for the better, she replied, "I've been here a year and nowhere have I felt so constricted, so circumvented, so restrained. Never have I been so unhappy."

At dinner that same evening the pretty young wife of a first secretary in a Scandinavian Embassy said to me, "It's the shopping that defeats me."

When I asked if she spoke Russian, her answer was that she did. "As I have no nurse for my little boy, I must take him to the shops with me," she explained, "and as I must go from queue to queue, he is buffeted about, stepped on and made to feel a nuisance."

"But can't you leave him in your car with your driver?"

"We have no car or driver. I shop by bus and that's not easy either, for they are always crowded and I stand a large part of the time."

At that same dinner another woman, the wife of a military attaché from a Middle Eastern country, when I asked about her shopping problems answered, "I have none. I shop by telephone and all of my things are delivered to my flat."

When I related the complaint of the Nordic housewife, she said, "I want to be fair. There is an extra charge for orders placed by telephone. Perhaps Madame cannot afford this."

I told a newspaper friend about the complaints I had heard about shopping and he said, "Shopping is hell. Our maid and I have tried the telephone-delivery system. We got very poor quality food and, on a number of occasions, we were short-weighted."

He asked me the name of the woman who was pleased with the telephone shopping service and when I told him, he screwed up his face and said, "I hope you will never have to eat a meal at her house. Her food is terrible."

I told him it was my experience that people who serve bad meals manage to serve them that way no matter the quality of the food.

"I agree," he said, "but food as terrible as hers must be eaten to be believed. I'm convinced the shops know she'll put up with anything—and send her anything. Anyway, her case is not typical. I think you got a truer picture from the other women."

"From a westerner's point of view."

"Of course," he agreed.

I did not have the opportunity of sampling the satisfied housewife's bill of fare, which was beside the point anyway. I was determined to go shopping myself, and some time later my wife and I spent two days at it.

One of the principal jobs of a diplomat on foreign assignment is, of course, to report and interpret and, wherever possible, anticipate the government's policies and moves. With meagre contact with high officialdom, with no opposition party, with the Soviet press and other communications media being instruments of the government, the members of the foreign Diplomatechisky Corpus do an amazingly sound job. I think they are especially competent when you consider that they have to reach many conclusions by an exchange of information, ideas, reports, rumors and sheer gossip. At the highest level, I found sharp differences of opinion on a number of vital subjects. Chief among these were the actual leadership in the Soviet Union, and the actual state of relations between the U.S.S.R. and Communist China.

I went to one luncheon party at the Moscow home of an envoy from a continental European nation, a man with considerable experience of the Soviet Union and other Eastern European Communist governments. Another guest was the ambassador of a small European country closely allied with the West. They asked me the question which I seemed to be answering wherever I went. What was the biggest change I had found?

"Without any question," I replied, "the disappearance of police terror. I don't want to be a bore about this, but I think that to fully appreciate how much better off the people are, one should have lived here during those last terrible years of Stalin."

"Tell me," asked one of the ambassadors, "I have a grown son here. He goes out with Russian friends all the time. He goes into their homes and he says their conversations cover just about everything. Now tell me, could that have happened during your earlier days here, Gilmore?"

"No, it couldn't. May I ask you, how do your son and his Russian friends amuse themselves?"

"They go to the theatre, to the cinema. They have parties in one another's flats. Why, last night my son came home exhausted from doing the Twist."

"Do they talk politics?"

"At the age of twenty-one did you talk politics?"

"No, I must confess I didn't, but then I wasn't the son of a foreign diplomat assigned to another foreign country."

"Perhaps, perhaps." He changed the subject.

I turned to the other ambassador. I knew he had two grown children.

"What about yours?" I asked. "Do they see many Russians their own age?"

"They have superficial contacts," he answered. "You see, the Soviets still have an approved list of people who can associate with foreigners. Granted the list has been tremendously enlarged since the years of Stalin, still, most of my contacts are approved contacts, and I'm afraid most of those of my children are too. Let me say this though. Once the contact with the foreigner has been made, some of them project it pretty far."

"That's refreshing," I said.

"I quite agree, but I want to emphasize that neither my children nor I have any free and easy contact with individual Russians."

"But I tell you my boy does," insisted the other ambassador.

"I'm quite sure he does. I simply want to answer Gilmore. Mine don't—and it's not from not trying."

I raised the subject of collective leadership in the U.S.S.R.

"I'm sure there is collective leadership," said one of the men. "I have absolute proof of this."

"Proof?" I asked, somewhat surprised.

"Yes, but I'm afraid I can't go into detail. You will have to believe me."

The other ambassador said he could not agree with his colleague. He mentioned the name of a former American envoy to Moscow, a man well known as an authority on the Soviet Union.

"I had a difference of opinion with him over collective leadership," said my host. "I insisted there was no collective leadership here." My host took a long draw on his cigar and turning to me said, "Your ambassador—and by that I mean the American Ambassador—insisted that Russia was being run like, to use his own expression, General Motors."

"I agree with that," said the other envoy.

"Well, I didn't and I don't," said our host. "I think it was about a year after the General Motors theory that the Ambassador came to me and told me he had been wrong. He agreed that it's impossible to run this country with a collective; that you must have a strong man at the top who makes most of the decisions."

"And Mr. Khrushchev is such a man?" I asked.

"He is, indeed."

"I'm sorry, but I can't go along with you," said Ambassador Number Two.

"Well," laughed the host, "one of these days I'll try to convince you."

Both men agreed that Mrs. Khrushchev had weighty influence with her husband.

"A moderating influence," said one. "It's been proven time and again."

When I asked him to go into detail, he replied that it would be easier if he gave me a paper he had written on the subject. Our hostess and two other ambassadorial wives who had been with Tamara then entered the room.

"Enough politics, enough," said one of them.

Later, over coffee, someone mentioned the late John Foster Dulles.

"You know," said my host, "Khrushchev respected Dulles."

"That's a surprise," I said.

"Perhaps, but in my presence Mr. Khrushchev once said that Dulles was an intelligent man, and a great American patriot."

"He never let Mr. Dulles know that opinion, did he?" I asked.

"No, I'm afraid he didn't."

11. On the
Train to Volgograd

I have always believed that the Soviet Army's defense of Moscow and its counter-offensive in the deep snows outside the capital in the brutally cold weather of December 1941–January 1942—considered as parts of a single operation—was a greater military triumph than the victory at Stalingrad the following winter. Yet it was the smashing success of the latter battle on the Volga that captured the attention of the world, as the turning point of World War II.

A handful of Western generals have, from time to time, sought to detract from the Soviet accomplishment in the ruins and rubble of that strangely shaped industrial city on the high west, or right bank of the Volga. Stalingrad was, in the days of the fighting, as now, only a little more than two miles wide while forty-four miles in length, a straggling settlement whose environs cling to the wide sluggish river like ivy to a wall. To suggest that the victory at Stalingrad was not a major exploit of arms is monstrously unfair and unworthy of an ally, but I suppose one did have to be there to judge the full impact of the Russian achievement and the degree of disaster for the then proud and seemingly invincible German Army.

Why the men in the Kremlin did not make more out of the triumph at the gates of Moscow, when they hurled back over two hundred enemy divisions, has always been something of a puzzle. Cautious of victory claims—at least in the early part of the war—the Soviet High Command, I believe, played it safe and took no chances. Although they dislodged the Germans from their extended positions around Moscow and sent them in full retreat to positions fifteen miles west of Mozhaisk, I felt then and feel now that Stalin and his commanders feared that another all-out effort by Hitler to capture Moscow might follow when the weather improved. Thus it was more prudent not to make too many claims and wave too many flags until the overall situation became clearer. Excessive victory communiqués might have enraged Hitler into mounting a massive air attack on Moscow. With its numerous wooden buildings and houses, the Soviet capital offered an enticing target for a fire raid. On top of everything else, it is a characteristic of the Slavs— never to tempt the gods. Stalin was no Slav, but being a secretive mountain man, he too shrank from flying too many pennants in the fickle winds of heaven. At Stalingrad, the victory was complete and the prisoners taken so numerous that there was no chance of tempting the dark and unseen forces in which many a Soviet citizen—including members of the Communist Party—believe. Then there was the name of the city on the Volga, the importance of which should not be discounted. It was named after the Leader and Teacher; it was his city. In his insanity of self-exaltation, Stalin undoubtedly attached great importance to insuring that it never fell to the hated invader. It is ironic that the Russians themselves have changed its name.

Before leaving London I had asked my travel agents if my wife and I could visit Stalingrad, or Volgograd as it is now called. I said we particularly wanted to be there during the victory celebrations. After several exchanges between London and Moscow, a trip to Volgograd was agreed upon.

We had been in Moscow for about a week when Intourist informed me that I had two reservations for a train that would leave about midnight on January 30th, reaching Volgograd about 7:30 o'clock the following evening. I received this notification about noon on the day of departure. As we were walking down the fifth floor corridor of the National behind a porter carrying our luggage, I felt a strange twinge in my left big toe, and I suppose my face revealed the pain, for Tamara asked, "What's the matter?"

I burst out laughing.

"What's so funny?" she demanded as I limped along.

"It's so ironical it's funny."

"I don't understand."

"Of course, you don't. But in this land of the so-called common man, in a country that prides itself on the proletariat being king, I'm afraid I'm about to come down with the disease of kings—gout."

"What's gout and what's it got to do with kings?"

"I've always been told that gout comes from high living. You know, too much pheasant and rich old port. Well, we've been living in gouty old England for the last nine years or so——"

By now we had reached the elevator.

"And you've had your share of the port if not the pheasant," said my wife.

"Yet I've never had gout before, and that's what I think I've got. It hurts like hell."

"Where?"

"My big toe. The big toe on my left foot."

"Perhaps we'd better call off the trip."

"Too late for that. Anyhow, I can be treated for gout in Volgograd as well as I can in Moscow, I suppose."

"You're sure you have the gout?"

"I can't remember stumping my toe on anything. That's what it feels like."

Loaded into a chauffeur-driven automobile and accompanied by an efficient and helpful Intourist official, we headed for the Kazansky Railway Station, and upon arriving at this small but busy terminal, it was immediately evident that in addition to the Gilmores, scores of Soviet Army officers were taking the Volgograd train. All about us were men in uniform, most of them of high rank.

We were led to Car B and upon entering the door, the first person I saw was Marshal Nikolai Voronov, the Soviet Army's top artillery commander. He looked little different than he did in the war years, a tall, broad-shouldered, large-nosed man with a large, friendly smile. Somehow, he reminded me of a cannon. To my utter surprise, I discovered that the Marshal and his aide, a Lieutenant Colonel, were in the four-berthed compartment for which I held two tickets. A female *provodnik* who was making up a pair of the beds said as she saw me, "Oh, yes, you've been moved."

I quite understood.

Midway down the sleeping car into which we were ushered, a large, darkish, balding man in the uniform of a Colonel was holding a light-hearted discussion with a white-haired motherly looking woman who possessed a strong featured but kindly face. They looked up and greeted us. By now my toe was causing much pain and overhearing a remark I made to Tamara, the woman said, "You seem to be suffering. Don't you want something to kill the pain?"

"Yes," I said, "but I'm afraid I have nothing."

"Just a moment," she said as she rummaged in a large black bag. Finding what she was looking for, she handed me two white pills and said, "Take one now and another before you go to sleep. You'll find them very effective against pain."

I thanked her and introduced us.

They introduced themselves and we all shook hands. I did not catch the Colonel's name, but I got hers—Shchors.

"The wife of the General?" I asked.

"Yes."

"We're delighted to know you."

"I'm pleased to know you."

She shook hands again and after exchanging a few meaningless pleasantries, Madame Shchors and the Colonel excused themselves, saying they were going to take a walk before the train departed.

"She's the wife, or the widow, I should say, of the late General Nikolai Shchors," I told Tamara. "If I remember correctly, he commanded a front for the Red Army during the Civil War. In any case, he was an extremely well known revolutionary and a close friend of Lenin's."

"She's nice," said Tamara.

In mounting pain I climbed into an upper berth, for it was obvious that the General's widow and the Colonel had taken one lower and one upper, leaving us the other pair.

In all my past travels in the Soviet Union, I had never before by accident found myself in a compartment on a train with a strange woman. With other men, yes. As I lay in my bunk I contemplated how I would dress and undress in such cramped surroundings. While I was trying to work out a solution for this dilemma, the two Russians returned and Madame Shchors said to me, "You know, you'll be a lot more comfortable if you remove your tie and jacket and your vest."

I thanked her and replied that I usually did not remove my jacket and vest while wearing suspenders. Saying this, I exhibited my pair of bright yellow British braces.

"Instead of being embarrassed," she replied with a quick smile, "I'm delighted you've got them on. They're a guarantee against real embarrassment. I mean, with them your trousers can't fall down."

With that remark the train gave a shudder, then a jerk and slowly we left for Volgograd. It was just about midnight and the four of us began talking of many things, as Russians do on trains.

I was aware that the Colonel was asking Tamara one question after another, all very politely, of course. Finally he said, "Are you English or American?"

"I have an American passport," Tamara told him.

"See here," he came back. "I've met many foreigners, but I've never met one who speaks Russian as well as you do."

"Thank you. You mean I have no accent?"

"Just a trace of one," said he.

"Oh, go on and tell him," I told Tamara.

"Tell him about what?" This from Madame Shchors.

"I was born in Russia," said Tamara.

"Of course, I knew it," beamed the Colonel.

"But you said I had a trace of a foreign accent."

"You do. You must have picked it up somewhere. Where were you born in Russia?"

"Moscow."

"Of course. That's it," said Madame Shchors. "You have a Moscow accent."

Out came those inevitable photographs. Tamara produced hers, Madame Shchors hers and the Colonel exhibited a set. They were all photographs of children and in Madame Shchors' case, pictures of children and grandchildren.

As I knew it would, the conversation at last turned to religion and the officer and the General's widow both explained how they did not believe in God.

"We do," said Tamara.

"He does not exist," said Madame Shchors, and coming from the mouth of one who resembled everybody's grandmother, the denial seemed strangely out of place.

"Our astronauts have proven that God does not exist," said Madame.

"How's that?" I asked from my perch in the upper berth.

"Why, when our astronauts were up there in the heavens circling the earth," she replied with what I thought was a faint smile, "they saw everything there was to see and they didn't see God!"

"Well," said I, "I guess that's strong evidence."

While we talked, a number of officers in uniform passed our door and two or three of them looked in and passed a few words of greeting.

"I'm absolutely astounded by this train," I said at last.

"Why?" asked the Colonel.

"I should have said that I'm astounded by being on this train. It seems that half the Soviet Army is aboard."

"I think our travelling companions on this car include three Marshals and at least three Generals," said the Colonel.

"Unbelievable," I told him.

"Why unbelievable?"

"My being on this train with them. I mean I'm a foreigner and an American journalist at that."

"Why not?" asked the Colonel, a little too glibly I thought. "You've got a ticket and this is a free country."

"In Stalin's day—when I was last here—I would not have been allowed within five hundred yards of this train."

"Many things have changed since Stalin," said Madame, "and all of it for the better."

"Do you agree, Colonel?"

"Absolutely."

Later, from what she intimated more than from what she said, I gathered this handsome, intelligent woman, the widow of a national hero, had been a prisoner of both the Germans and Joseph Stalin, at one time or another, but I pressed her on neither point.

"By profession," she said, "I'm an engineer. When I was younger, I used to put on trousers just like a man and do a man's work."

I complimented her.

"I was only doing my duty as a Soviet citizen."

Here I felt was a true revolutionary, one of the old school, passionately but not bumptiously devoted to what she defined as the ideals of Lenin.

I cannot recall what led to the subject, but we began discussing punishment, Madame Shchors saying she believed that all wrong-doers should be punished and punished severely.

"Come now," asked the Colonel of Tamara, "you're a former Soviet citizen who has lived for ten years in capitalist countries, what do you think about punishment?"

"Oh, it would take too long to tell you."

"Then sum it up. I'm very curious to hear your views, Tamara Adamovna."

"Yes, do tell us, please," asked Madame.

"I believe in the teaching of Christ. That it is better to turn the other cheek."

Asked what I thought, I answered that I believed in some forms of punishment, but I did not think that for every mistake there should be some punishment, adding rather grandly, I am afraid, "I don't like to play God as Stalin did."

"He played God, all right," agreed the Colonel.

Before leaving Moscow, through the kindness of a friend, I had armed myself with four bottles of Scotch whisky. I felt the time had come to produce one of them. The pill had eased my suffering and I felt that a whisky might make me sleep more easily.

"What is this?" asked the old revolutionary.

"Whisky," I replied.

Examining the bottle, her large grey eyes lit on the Royal Coat of Arms and the words, "By Appointment to Her Majesty Queen Elizabeth II."

"What's that?"

I tried to explain.

"You mean the English Queen drinks this stuff?"

I replied that I presumed she did—in moderation.

"Moderation or not, she should be ashamed of herself."

"But you're drinking it, Madame Shchors, and we're delighted that you are."

"Yes, but I'm no Queen."

How typically Russian, I thought to myself. I recalled the numerous times I had heard the very same sort of non-sequitur reaction from Mr. Andrei Vyshinsky and other Soviet spokesmen at the United Nations, not to Scotch whisky, of course, but to greater and even lesser matters.

"I want you to take another of these pills," ordered Madame Shchors. "Don't be afraid. My daughter is a doctor."

Again I thanked her and did as I was told.

When about half the contents of the bottle had been consumed, she announced she was going to sleep.

"Close your eyes, please," she said and I again did as I was told.

"So this is how it's done with mixed doubles," I said to myself.

Airplane crashes, train wrecks, mine cave-ins and explosions, the sinking of ships, earthquakes and other life-taking disasters are not news in the Soviet press—when they happen in the Soviet Union. Hence they are not reported, with rare exceptions. But let these calamities take place in the capitalist West, or even in the social democracies of Europe, and they become news. As a result of this policy, a great many inhabitants of the U.S.S.R. are convinced that their country is immune from such tragedies.

I have heard peasants and laborers and a few Komsomol zealots insist that it is the callous flint-hearted capitalist bosses, with no concern for the lives of their workers, who are responsible for such misfortunes and that therefore under Communism such adversities are impossible.

After one has lived and travelled in Russia for any length of time the mind seems to become conditioned to the infallibility of public transport. My thoughts were certainly far from anything of this sort as our train rumbled on towards Volgograd. As I lay on my bunk of pain from the gout, I was nearly thrown to the floor as the train ground to a quick and agonizing stop.

"What's happened?" said the Colonel from his perch across from mine.

"I can't imagine," I called back. "Perhaps we've hit something."

Silence.

"Or maybe something's hit us."

More silence.

"I'm going to investigate," said the officer, rolling out of his berth and opening our compartment door.

There was a commotion in the corridor and several people seemed to be asking the same question, "What's happened?"

One of the officers who had visited our cabin the night before stuck his head in the door.

"Do you know why we've stopped?" I asked.

"I can't imagine."

I repeated that perhaps we had hit something, but the officer shook his head and said, "I don't think it's anything like that. Our locomotive drivers are too clever and well trained."

"You mean you don't have train wrecks?"

"I've never heard of any."

"No airplane crashes?"

"None that I know of."

Soon the Colonel returned and announced that our train had hit a truck on a grade crossing.

"Anyone hurt?" I asked.

"Yes, the man who was driving the truck and a woman with him, but the child in the woman's arms was thrown clear. They've just lifted her out of a snow bank uninjured."

"I can't understand," said the other officer.

"The truck driver ran in front of the train," explained the Colonel.

"Ah," said the other officer.

"The truck's a ruin, but the two grown-ups and the baby are to be put in the baggage car. Fortunately there's a Major from the Medical Corps aboard, on his way to

Volgograd and he'll be looking after things until we get to the next big town."

"Then you do have accidents," I said.

"This isn't an accident," protested the officer who still hung about. "It's stupidity on the part of someone. Probably the truck driver. What's he doing anyway driving a woman and a baby in this kind of weather at this hour of the morning?"

"They're his wife and child," volunteered the Colonel. And then to me as if to wind up the subject of accidents, "How's your foot?"

"Maybe a bit better, thanks to Madame Shchors' medicine."

"You better take some more," she said. "I have plenty more. What are you doing about breakfast? The Colonel and I have plenty for us all."

I thanked her as graciously as I could, but explained Tamara and I would breakfast in the dining-car.

"But I tell you we have plenty."

"Of course," chimed in the Colonel. "We've got enough to feed half this car."

"Thank you. Thank you very much."

With some difficulty I got down from my berth and hobbled towards the lavatory. The crowded corridor sounded as if it had been taken over by a swarm of bees. At every electric plug—and there must have been at least a dozen—various officers were shaving themselves with electric razors. Ten years before I had never seen a Russian using one. I am sure they did not exist then in the U.S.S.R.

The lavatory was clean, but very wet. In their ablutions the Russians are enthusiastic and energetic, flinging the water about with gay abandon. For a long time "as cold as a Siberian toilet seat" has served as a graphic metaphor. For something being truly damp, I think "as wet as a toilet seat on a Russian train" would not be inappropriate.

While Tamara was washing—and throwing the water

about, I suppose—I got out my electric razor and joined the officers in the corridor. Like boys with new toys we discussed the merits of electric shaving.

"I would never go back to wet shaving," said a gruff old General. "I was always cutting myself. What about you?"

"I've never used anything but an electric razor for about twenty years," I told him.

Eyeing me suspiciously, he asked, "Where did you get one twenty years ago? We hadn't invented them then."

I do not like to argue before breakfast—especially in Russian—so I rationed my reply to, "They existed and I had one—in Moscow."

In the restaurant car up ahead we enjoyed fruit juice, fried eggs and ham. Our table was near the end of the car, beside a counter piled high with bottles of beer, wine, champagne and cognac. The time was 8:20 o'clock in the morning, but the bar was doing a brisk business and at tables about us everyone seemed to be drinking. We spent an hour or a bit more at breakfast and I was astounded at the purchase and consumption of alcoholic drink that went on non-stop.

"They're going to fight the Battle of Stalingrad all over again," said Tamara in English.

"If you'll excuse me," I said, "I think this is going to be the Bottle of Stalingrad."

No sooner had we returned to our compartment than our Russian friends began scolding us for not sharing their breakfast.

"You must promise to have lunch with us," said Madame Shchors.

"With the greatest of pleasure," said Tamara.

We finished another bottle of Scotch and started on another and I must admit that the cold chicken, ham, cheese and spiced sausage that the old revolutionary and the Colonel laid out for us were wonderful. It was only natural that we began singing, and as we were all on our way to celebrate a great World War II victory we sang the old war songs, such melodies as "Dear City," "Give Me a Smoke," "The Blue Handkerchief" and "Sasha."

The Colonel had a nice baritone and as he and Tamara knew all the words to every song, Madame Shchors and I did the harmony. During the vocalizing numerous officers— including a Marshal whose front I had visited during the war—dropped in, or wedged in, and joined the sing-song.

All this was incredible to me. Even during the war when security restrictions were relatively lax, I remembered no occasion when high-ranking Soviet officers lifted their voices in song with foreigners.

As I have said before, the hospitality and friendliness of the Russian people is boundless and each of these made us feel welcome and very much at home. The Marshal, who had been a General during that visit to the front, became sentimental and said—and for the life of me I cannot remember what led up to the remark, "America and the Soviet Union were allies in the last war. God forbid that we shall ever have another, but if we do, we shall be on the same side again. Your Pentagon is no friend of ours, but the American people and the Russian people will never fight one another because in the end it will be the people who decide things."

"You are right about the American people, *gospodin* Marshal," I said, "but don't forget, the Pentagon is made up of people too, and as our Pentagon sometimes provokes you, your government sometimes provokes us."

"Our government is a fair and just government. Our people are behind it."

"And the United States is a fair and just government and our people are behind it."

"Well, as you're a guest in our country, we won't argue about it," he said with a smile. "Come, let's drink to the everlasting friendship between the United States and the Soviet Union."

There must have been at least fifteen persons in or half-way in our compartment. With what appeared to be genuine enthusiasm, they all joined in the toast.

Soon the sun set and it grew dark.

"Only a few minutes more to go," announced Madame Shchors.

We sat very quiet looking out the window at the lights of Volgograd, and then as the train came to a stop at last we said our farewells. The old lady left us saying, "You must come and visit me in my apartment in Moscow. Promise?"

This was a new twist. In years past you met Russians—occasionally. But it was a rare occasion when they suggested you visit them in their homes.

Volgograd was unusually cold but a pretty girl from Intourist gave us a warm welcome and introduced herself as Svetlana. She took us by car to the modern Intourist Hotel overlooking the Square of the Fallen Warriors which I recalled was in the very heart of the city, and which had been in the center of the fighting.

After a hot bath, which made my foot feel better, we changed our clothes and went down to the large, too brightly illuminated dining-room for dinner. There we met a number of foreign correspondents—including two from Red China—who were in Volgograd for the official celebrations.

We lingered on until after midnight. Unsuccessfully, I tried to draw the Chinese into our conversation. They smiled politely and made only the most noncommital remarks in Russian.

"Have you been to Volgograd before?"

"No."

"How do you estimate the importance of the Russian victory here?"

"It was a good fight."

"Armies that deeply invade this country always lose."

"Do they?"

"Did you know that Russia has been invaded from the

East more frequently and more successfully than from the West?"

"Has it?"

"Yes, don't you remember your history?"

"Such history is not important."

"How do you like your job?"

"Excuse me, I must go to bed."

Deep bows all around.

Soon we also left the dining-room where the lights were so bright I felt as if I had been eating in a television studio.

Tamara walked, and I hobbled. As we went down the long corridor that led to our suite, song and laughter came from behind every door we passed. Outside the doors like squads of disorderly sentinels stood dozens of empty bottles and the carpeted corridor echoed with the quick thudding of waiters' feet as they sped along with trays loaded with bottled reinforcements.

"You said it," smiled Tamara. "The Bottle of Stalingrad. And why not?"

"Agreed."

12. The Scene of a Battle

Twenty years before, in the cellar of a building around the corner from what was now our hotel, Friedrich Paulus, a mediocre officer of the German General Staff, sat on a filthy camp bed staring at the blank wall before him.

"What," he asked in a stunned voice, "are we going to do?"

He appeared to address his remarks to the wall, but it was his Chief of Staff who replied, saying, "In God's name send for the Russians."

Only a few hours before he decided—against Hitler's orders—to give up the hopeless struggle in Stalingrad, Paulus had been elevated by the Fuehrer to the supreme post of Field Marshal and, in one of history's most unsubtle asides, the leader of the Third Reich added, "Never has a German Field Marshal surrendered."

For twenty-three weeks the Germans and the Soviets had battled over the center of this elongated town on the banks of the great Volga. They had fought from block to block, house to house and, in some cases, from floor to floor in buildings and houses.

From the basement of a building that overlooked a strategic square near the northern section of Stalingrad, a short and imaginative Red Army Sergeant named Jakob Pavlov and three soldiers held the house for fifty-eight days.

They lost track of the number of times they beat off German attacks, and cleared individual members of advance parties from the rooms of that building.

So resolute was Pavlov's defense and such a master was he of the situation that during the Battle of Stalingrad he became known as The House Manager, as indeed he certainly was.

Corpses littered hundreds of battered structures and the rubble around them, and conditions became so desperate for the encircled Germans that when supplies of food ran out many killed their horses and lived off them. As the last horse was eaten, Hitler's once proud troops were driven by their hunger to shooting and eating the rats that had been living off the corpses. It was the last act before cannibalism.

With the surrender of Paulus and another grouping in the southern sector of Stalingrad on January 31, 1943, and then the capitulation of a third pocket north of the city on February 2nd, the battle was over at last.

The Soviet High Command's last communiqué on Stalingrad said:

"Today (February 2nd) the forces of the Don Front broke the resistance of the enemy encircled north of Stalingrad and compelled them to capitulate. The last center of the enemy resistance in the Stalingrad area has thus been crushed. Today, February 2nd, 1943, the historic battle before Stalingrad has been concluded with the final victory of our forces."

It was the day following this final surrender that the Soviet authorities flew a few of us correspondents from Moscow to the still smoldering city battleground. I could smell the stench of death that still hung over the snowy battle scene, as German prisoners continued to straggle across the frozen Volga to imprisonment. Of the more than 125,000 men surrendered by Paulus, only about 5,000 returned to their homeland from Siberia.

I do not know who it was who first put the von before Paulus. I have no record of whether it was the Field Marshal or the Russians, but it was as Von Paulus that we met him.

At that time he was being kept prisoner in a wooden house on the outskirts of Stalingrad. We pressed our Soviet escorting officers for an opportunity to interview him and after some discussion with the Red Army commanders on this front, they took us to the Field Marshal's place of confinement.

Walking stiffly between two Red Army officers, he was brought to the large and deep veranda of the wooden house.

"You may question the Field Marshal," said one of the Russians.

"What is your name?" asked one of us in German.

"Friedrich von Paulus."

"Is it true that you defied Hitler's orders in surrendering?" was the second question put to him.

With a grunt, he slowly turned his back on us and without another word, disappeared into the house that was his prison.

I thought it odd at the time that the Soviets let him get away with refusing to be interviewed. Time and again on the front I had seen them take a very firm line with German prisoners who hesitated in answering questions asked by Soviet as well as Western newsmen. But the giving of his name was the beginning and the end of our interview with Paulus.

Later he was sent to Moscow in high style for those war years, in a first-class compartment of a well-heated train, and supplied with good food and wine. In the Soviet capital Paulus worked well for his captors and served them well. It was only then that I understood why they had handled him gently at Stalingrad after his surrender. The Soviet also referred to him as Von Paulus, rather than the less elegant Paulus. For a man who before the days of Stalingrad never commanded so much as a regiment in the field, he was an odd choice for a Field Marshal.

If Paulus told us nothing on that very cold day twenty years earlier, there was a Soviet officer who did. He was V. I. Chuikov, now a Field Marshal of the Soviet Army, a lucid speaker and one of the most intelligent officers I ever met in the U.S.S.R.

On the morning of February 1, 1963, I was to see Chuikov again. I met him in the corridor of my Volgograd hotel. We exchanged greetings and he professed to remember my visit to his headquarters twenty years before. I thought Chuikov looked remarkably unchanged by time.

Standing in that corridor, I was in excruciating pain. The pain and the swelling had spread from my big toe to my ankle and it was all I could do to keep my shoe on, unlaced of course. I had not returned to Volgograd to take to my bed and I insisted—pain or no pain—on seeing the new city built on the war's ruins.

I asked our Intourist guide if my wife and I and Reinhold Ensz, of our Moscow bureau, could have an automobile for sightseeing.

"Oh, I'm afraid that will be impossible," she said. "You see, the city is full of people who've come here for the celebration."

"Yes," I said, "we are three of them."

"I'm afraid all the cars have been taken, but you have an appointment with my chief at 10 o'clock" (it was then ten minutes before 10 o'clock), "and we shall see what we can do."

On the dot of ten the chief appeared, a small dark woman with close-cropped hair. She asked us what we would like to do while in Stalingrad and when I told her,

she answered, "All will be done and your car is now waiting for you."

Our status rose in the eyes of Svetlana, our guide, and
she skillfully escorted us around the city. So indelibly was
the name of Stalingrad stamped on the minds of everyone
that Svetlana, I thought, could be forgiven for one or two
times when she unconsciously referred to Volgograd as
Stalingrad.

First we drove to the bank overlooking the Volga, now
choked by ice blocks. My memory flew back to my original
visit to this very spot. It was during the hot dusty summer of
1942 when I stopped in Stalingrad on a trip down the Volga
from Kuibyshev. My destination was Astrakhan on the
Caspian Sea. This was, of course, before the Battle of Stalingrad, but even then, the German army was rapidly advanc-
ing from the west.

In twenty years the Soviets had done a vast amount of re-
building and together with the construction of the nearby
Don-Volga Canal, it was impressive. For years the rulers
of Russia had been intrigued with the idea of a canal con-
necting the two rivers where, near Stalingrad, they are but
thirty-eight miles apart. In 1950, the sixty mile long canal
was completed. A hydro-electric station was finished in
1960.

Remembering that I had seen photographs of a huge
statue of Stalin at the entrance to the canal, I asked Svetlana
what had happened to it.

"It's gone," was her terse reply. She hurried us on.

During the fighting, more than 25,000 apartment houses
were destroyed in Stalingrad. From what I could tell, most
of them had been rebuilt. On the edges of the city, however,
there still remained scores of small wooden homes.

We drove out to Mamai Kurgan, a high flat-topped hill
with a commanding view of the whole Volgograd area.
This had once been the capital of the Tatar Prince Mamai.
Before us was the Red October Factory, scene of day and
night fighting during the Stalingrad campaign.

"No pictures here, please," cautioned our guide, and when Ensz plunked his camera on the seat beside her as he got out of the car, Svetlana observed to me, "I see he's making a demonstration."

We capped our tour of the city with a visit to the great square outside our hotel, in the center of which Nikita Khrushchev, a leading member of the Military Council of Stalingrad during the fighting twenty years earlier had made a stirring speech on February 4.

I remember seeing Khrushchev at Stalingrad at the time, but I could not recall actually hearing him make the speech. I do not mean to suggest that he did not make it, but although I remember reading it, it caused no great stir at the time. In those days, neither I nor anyone else—including the most powerful of Soviet officials—had the faintest idea that this man would become Stalin's successor.

It had been a long morning and a cold one and I was delighted to get back to the hotel. It was especially rewarding, for in the lobby we met Sergeant Pavlov, the House Manager of the Battle of Stalingrad. He was a smallish man with broad shoulders, dark hair and grey-green eyes. After being introduced, he kindly agreed to answer some questions. A more modest man I never met, but modesty is a characteristic often encountered in the simplest of Russians.

Asked what he remembered most about the fifty-eight days and nights he spend defending that house, he replied, "Our phonograph. We had one in the basement and I became an expert in winding it."

Someone inquired if there had not also been a piano in the basement and he said, "Yes, I played it a lot too, but I've never been as expert on the piano as I became on winding the phonograph. I'm a master at that."

A group of us were putting questions to him, and when someone inquired what he was now doing, he replied that he was a house builder.

"Don't you ever wreck any houses?" one of us asked.

With fine irony, he replied, "I think the world has had enough of that. What we need to do is build houses."

Pavlov and his tiny wife had come to Volgograd as honored guests for the twentieth anniversary celebrations.

There are almost as many theories about the causes of gout as there are ways of making mint juleps. It is brought on, I have been told, by over-indulgence in food and/or alcohol, an operation, an injury, an emotional upset, an acute infection, or even a change in the weather.

Philosophers, it seems, are prone to gout for it grabbed Hippocrates by one of his big toes as far back as the Fifth Century B.C. Three hundred years later, Seneca blamed it on high living and pointed out that women could be gouty as well as men. The vintage years for gout, however, appear to have been the eighteenth and nineteenth centuries, and a lot of the blame for it was laid on John Methuen, English diplomat and Lord Chancellor of Ireland, who initiated the Methuen Treaty whereby the rich port of Portugal replaced French wines as the class drink in Great Britain.

Gout has been—rightly or wrongly—identified with high-living. It seemed ironical in the extreme to have contracted it not in affluent Britain, but in the Soviet Union whose living standard, though greatly improving, is still far behind that of the West. So be it, I had it.

As a group of us assembled in the lobby of the Intourist Hotel, preparatory to attending a wreath-laying and flame-lighting in the Square of the Fallen Warriors, I was suffering to a degree that made my walk a hobble and every step a stabbing pain. My left foot was twice its normal size and throbbing.

Just before we were shepherded into a cold of fifteen degrees below zero Fahrenheit, I noticed that I was not the only person suffering from locomotion trouble. Supported by an aide, a florid-face Marshal, who shall be nameless, was assisted through the lobby. The Marshal, built along the classical model for high-ranking Soviet commanders, must have weighed two hundred thirty pounds, and he listed, staggered and dragged his feet on his way to the ceremony, shifting a large proportion of his weight on to his aide who, fortunately, happened to be a robust young man. The Marshal's grey caracul slid off his head as he reached the front door and with the dexterity of an acrobat, the aide managed to keep his boss upright and recover his cap at the same time.

Feeling as if my whole left leg was a boil, I left the hotel supported by Tamara and a walking stick I had secured in Volgograd. To curious onlookers—and there was a big crowd in the Square of the Fallen Warriors—the Marshal and I were an amusing side attraction.

The ceremony was brief and impressive. Several Party officials and commanders spoke eloquently, I thought, of the Red Army men and citizens of Stalingrad who had given their lives in defense of the city on the Volga.

That evening, with the pain increasing, I managed, and again with Tamara's assistance, to attend the official memorial meeting commemorating the twentieth anniversary of the great victory on the Volga.

Most of the heroes of Stalingrad were up on the stage, Marshals Chuikov, A. I. Yeremenko, Voronov and Colonel Generals Rudemstiev and Shumilov. Yeremenko, a genial man as well as a good speaker, was given an outstanding ovation when he announced the day was a double anniversary for him—the Stalingrad victory and his fiftieth year of being a soldier.

There were three outstanding features of the long evening—the complete omission of Stalin's name, for not a speaker made the slightest reference to him; the solemnity of the occasion and the tears in so many eyes; and the well-dressed state of the audience, particularly that of the men. In that large auditorium the men were in dark, well-cut suits, white shirts (some with French cuffs, I noted) and dark ties. Gone were the bell-bottomed trousers and long floppy sleeves of yesterday, and the flamboyant ties with knots the size of hen eggs.

"And strange," I said to myself, "the absence of Khrushchev."

As I had a story to file, I excused myself to my Soviet hosts and hobbled back to the hotel and dictated to Moscow a fairly longish account of the formal observance of the anniversary of a battle that will be remembered, I suppose, as long as military history is written.

Watching me drag myself to bed, Tamara said, "I don't care what you say, I'm calling in a doctor tomorrow morning. You can't go on like this."

"Well, we'll see," I told her.

Over my portable radio I listened from my bed to the remainder of the ceremony and, satisfied that I had missed nothing newsworthy, slipped off to sleep with my throbbing foot propped on a pair of pillows.

The following morning Intourist produced not only a doctor but a specialist, the latter being a large motherly woman in a white apron and white headdress. She asked a few questions in a soft gentle voice, spent many minutes examining my foot and finally pronounced that I was suffering from a severe attack of *podagra* (gout).

I told her that my gout was vivid testimony of the improvement in the living standards of the Soviet Union.

"Food," she replied, "has nothing to do with *podagra*. Neither does drink. Extreme cold and exposure has brought this on, together, I would say, with some strong emotion."

I wondered—but I thanked her profusely.

"Don't worry," she smiled, "we'll have you up in a few hours."

Excusing herself, the specialist disappeared for thirty or forty minutes and then marched into the room with medicines and bandages which, applied carefully and professionally, brought me almost instant relief.

I thanked her and asked, "Well, how much do I owe you for all this trouble and these medicines and so on?"

"Charges?" She looked downright startled. "There are no charges. I have only been doing my duty."

"Is your duty to look after some gouty foreigner?"

"My duty is to heal the sick."

She reached down and lightly poking me in the ribs said, "You're better already. I'll come back to see you later."

"What should I eat?" I asked.

"Anything you like."

"And drink?"

"Nothing alcoholic."

"Then alcohol is bad for *podagra* after all?"

"It has nothing to do with alcohol and alcohol has nothing to do with *podagra*. Alcohol just happens to be bad for anyone."

"I'll never understand Russians," I said.

"Originally," said the man in the restaurant, "this city became great because of Stalin." His face was furrowed in frowns. "Then, after the great victory of Stalingrad," he went on, "Stalin became great because of this city." He looked the picture of dejection as he added, "Now it's all gone . . . gone . . . and we're nothing." He began to cry.

The name-changing of this city forms a neat and curious footnote to history. This big bustling city of nearly a million persons for four days actually existed without a name.

Think of the situation in terms of one's home town. How would it be to grow up a New Yorker, a Londoner, a Chicagoan, a San Franciscan, or Houstonian, and then suddenly, overnight, to discover that one was living in a place without a name and without identification? For four days and nights you do not know your city's name. In the twentieth century this must be a unique situation.

"It was a strange feeling," said A. A. Pushkarev, a dental assistant. "Nobody told us anything. Nothing was explained. The newspapers didn't come out. The radio and television said nothing. We were confused and dumbfounded. We didn't know what to do. What did you put at the top of a letter? What did you tell your children? What did you say to your neighbor?"

Odd things began happening on the morning of November 5, 1961. The inhabitants of Stalingrad awakened to find that the thirty-foot statue of Stalin overlooking the Square of the Fallen Warriors in the heart of the city had vanished. In its place was a large empty base. Down at the entrance to the Don-Volga Canal, another massive statue of the dictator who ruled the lives of these and all other Soviet people for twenty-five years had gone.

Yet the city was still Stalingrad. Then, in the early morning of November 7, the large sign STALINGRAD at each end of the city's railway station disappeared. The mysterious powers at work during the night and early morning also mounted the roof of the then new Stalingrad Hotel. Apparently aware of what was up—or perhaps merely carrying out instructions—they removed the STALIN part of the large illuminated sign.

"It was strange yet comic," recalled Alexei L. Klemov as I pieced together this story of Volgograd. "I remember looking up and seeing the sign that simply read GRAD. That didn't make much sense, did it?"

Life in what had been Stalingrad slowed to a near halt. Some people did not go to work and children stayed away from schools. Despite Stalin, there was great civic pride in the city that bore his name. Every man, woman and child knew that this city, the one he called home, was known all over the world; that statesmen of many countries claimed that the victory at Stalingrad turned the tide of World War II. Did not tourists come from many lands to visit Stalingrad, to see the city that rose from its own ruins to become a modern metropolis, and visit the battlefields as they visited the battlefields of France after the first World War? Yet overnight its proud name had vanished and it had become a nameless place, an unidentified spot on the map that was not even dignified by being called X.

On the morning of November 11, the local newspaper published the announcement that from then on, Stalingrad would be known as Volgograd. In the de-Stalinization that was sweeping the country the name-changing was, of course, understandable, but it would have been more understandable if the inhabitants of Stalingrad had been given an opportunity of expressing their opinion about the name of the place in which they lived.

"God knows I feared and hated Stalin," said Galya Batalova, a skilled worker in a local factory, "but Stalingrad to me had become bigger than Stalin. I didn't associate the name of my city with the man."

Without knowing exactly why, a number of inhabitants told me they became indignant at the way things were handled, but balanced reporting must also record the fact that many welcomed the change and had no complaint, or at least, made none when I asked them for their opinion.

"Frankly, I don't care what they called it," said a railway worker T. O. Filipov. "The good thing was the removal of Stalin's statues. He'd been dead for eight years, but seeing him up there, staring down on you, well, it made a lot of us uncomfortable."

To give him his due, Stalin played an important role in the young Red Army's victory here during the terrible months of the Civil War. He also had much to do with the victory over Hitler's armies in 1943. His positive contributions are still on record in Volgograd's historical museum, but there is no emphasis on them.

Today the emphasis is where it should be—on the magnificent performance of the Red Army officers and soldiers, and the gallantry and sufferings of the Soviet people during the siege of Stalingrad.

Mr. Khrushchev also made a significant contribution to the victory over Paulus. As a general in uniform he spent much time in Stalingrad and the Stalingrad area when some of it was under fire. He was an energetic and vital member of the Military Council of Stalingrad, the group of Communist

Party officials and army commanders who forged the victory.

From what I could learn, Khrushchev has rejected numerous proposals to erect a statue to him in Volgograd. With becoming modesty he has played down his part in the victory. Perhaps this was why he remained in Moscow and did not go to Volgograd for the twentieth anniversary celebration, leaving the stage to the military commanders and the local authorities.

There was another reaction to the name change that I think should be reported. I met a young woman who was born in the city when it was Stalingrad and who is living and working there now it is Volgograd. "At least," she said, "they named it after a river and not after a man. I'm getting sick of our cities being named after men. Why not a woman sometime?"

To mark the end of the anniversary celebrations a mammoth salute was mounted over Volgograd. It was the same sort of pyrotechnic display the Soviets employed during the war to celebrate major victories on the front, and as a correspondent stationed in Moscow, I had witnessed them by the hundreds.

On this night—our last in Volgograd—Tamara and I stood at our hotel window watching the many-colored lights carve arches in the cold night sky.

"Does all that remind you of anything?" asked my wife.

"Yes, Vicki."

"I thought you'd say that."

"Let's see. How long ago was that?"

"She'll be nineteen on August 14."

Nineteen years ago our first child was born in a Moscow hospital while the same sort of lights showered over the capital marking some Red Army victory.

In those days, I in company with nearly everyone else in much-suffering Moscow, possessed no automobile and when it became alarmingly apparent that Tamara's child was about to be born, I became desperate. The hospital to which she had been assigned was about seven or eight miles from where we lived, the hour was about two in the morning and such things as taxis or ambulances for expectant mothers just did not exist. I played my ace and woke up the United States Ambassador, W. Averell Harriman. He answered the telephone and when he understood my plight, his words were, "Don't worry. My car'll be there as quickly as I can get the chauffeur dressed."

Mr. Harriman is a man of action and he gets action out of those around him. Mr. Harriman's Russian driver, with the ambassadorial machine, was at our front door in less than ten minutes.

With that morning still in mind, I said, "My God, a lot's happened since then, hasn't it?"

"It surely has, hoaney."

"A war's been won. Stalin has died. I got you and Vicki out. . . ."

"What about Susanna?"

"Got you and Vicki and Susanna out," I corrected myself, for a second daughter had been born to us during my residence in Moscow.

"And God has given us a third daughter, little Natasha," broke in Tamara, "and Vicki's looking after Susanna and Natasha this very night."

"You know the date?" I asked.

"Yes, it's Natasha's sixth birthday."

"We must send her a telegram," I said.

"I've already done it. She's having a big birthday party. I made all the arrangements before we left London."

"Thank you, darling."

"Don't thank me. That's what mothers are for."

"Thank you just the same."

"How's the gout?"

"Better. As the professor said, much better."

"Hoaney, would you ever like to come back and live and work in Russia again?"

"I don't know. I'd have to think about that for a long time. What about you?"

"Like you. I also don't know."

There was a long silence.

"Hoaney, am I going to have any trouble getting out of here? Every time I think about the children, and that's pretty often, I worry."

"Of course you'll have no trouble," I said with what I hoped sounded like assurance.

We left it at that.

13. From Rostov
to Tiflis

The following morning we were up and dressed by 6:30. We had been instructed that we must leave for the Volgograd airport at 7:30. Thanks to the splendid woman specialist, I could actually walk without pain once more. Down in the lobby we learned that fog in Volgograd and Rostov-on-Don, our next destination, was holding up the plane and that it would not take off on schedule. So we had breakfast and then returned to our room. At 1 P.M. we were assured there was little chance of the plane taking off for Rostov that day, so philosophically we shrugged off the thought of delay and ordered a large lunch.

We had finished the first course when Svetlana entered the dining-room and said the plane would be departing for Rostov-on-Don after all.

"But," she assured us, "you have plenty of time to finish your meal."

Ten minutes later the maitre d'hotel, one Ivan Ivanovich, marched up to the table, announced the plane was waiting for us and gave us a lecture, the theme of which was—never order a big meal when you are waiting for a plane to take off.

I almost exploded, but when I saw Svetlana's anxious face in the doorway, I swallowed my anger, but not the rest of the meal, and hurried out to the waiting car.

We purred through deep snows to the airport, twelve miles from the town, and there we saw that the plane was being held for us, and the stares and glares of the people who were to be our fellow-passengers to Rostov, indicated they had been waiting for some time.

The foreigner, I remarked to myself, may be confused and inconvenienced through inefficiency and bureaucracy in Russia, but he is still treated as an honored guest. In my homeland would a regularly scheduled airline flight be delayed for a Soviet newspaperman and his wife? Hardly.

The ninety minute trip to Rostov in an ancient DC-4 was bumpy but uneventful and we were met by a smiling, very blue-eyed blonde named Leila and her Intourist colleague Valerey, a young man in a smartly tailored short jacket, narrow and cuffless slacks. Both Leila and Valerey spoke excellent English.

"I'm afraid," cautioned Leila, "you won't find our hotel as up to date as the one you've been staying in in Volgograd." This proved to be the understatement of our entire trip.

Room 207 in an ancient hostelry on Rostov's main street, was a spacious musty horror with a gleaming white refrigerator in the living room, a small curtained sleeping compartment and a smelly private bathroom with a badly warped toilet seat.

Leaving Tamara at the hotel, Leila and I went on a sight-seeing tour of Rostov-on-Don, and noting the vast amount of new construction, I told myself that the old hotel and the scalloped toilet seat were, after all, unimportant.

During the war, Rostov changed hands four times and, despite the tragedies and suffering, it gave rise to a famous cartoon. This showed an elderly Russian railway laborer at work on a section of track within the much-occupied city. Presumably every time the city changed hands, the railway gauge changed too, for Russia maintains a wide-gauge track whereas Germany and continental Europe use narrow-gauge. Armed with a long cold crowbar, the Russian toiler was muttering to himself, "Wide gauge, narrow gauge, narrow gauge, wide gauge, wide gauge, narrow gauge—my God, I'm going nuts."

It was dark when Leila and I returned to the hotel, but as we had had little lunch we decided to dine early. The dining-room was a setting from a Chekhov play and some of the diners were real Chekhovian characters. The band was Soviet Provincial Modern, and it struck up as if it were chasing an army of enemies, growing louder and faster with each bar. Through aching ears I finally recognized Billy Strayhorn's "Take the A Train." This was followed by two Russian tunes, played as loud and fast as the other. At last, the band seemed to run out of steam, for the volume and tempo dropped while they played something I felt must be "Smoke Gets in Your Eyes."

At the next table sat a girl who must have been one of the belles of Rostov-on-Don, a short curvy cutie with a stylish green dress, her brown hair in a bee-hive pile above her pretty face. With her was a handsomely dressed young man who possessed, of all things, a derby or bowler hat. Later we fell to talking, and extremely curious over where he had found this highly un-Soviet piece of haberdashery, I inquired its origin.

"I ordered it from England," he said very casually.

More Russians joined us and one of them, another well-turned out young man, was the first and only Russian I ever met who did not like classical music.

"Hitler adored classical music," he observed. "I think that's why he was crazy."

I asked him what sort of music he liked and his reply was, "Kule djhazz."

This was not the only surprise of an unusual evening.

The band, once more playing loud and fast, rattled the dishes with a musical cannonade that occasionally sounded like something I had heard before. I got up and walking to the elevated bandstand asked the leader what he was playing.

"*Olmiss,*" he said.

"Excuse me, will you say that again?"

"*Olmiss,*" he repeated. When he saw I still did not understand, he handed me a piece of sheet music.

To my delight the tune was "Ole Miss," a song about a train in the deep South of the U.S. For years it was a favorite with bands playing traditional jazz.

Back at our table, one of our newly-made friends asked me if I knew the definition of an optimist.

"Yes," I brightened, delighted at the opportunity of being able to inject a small political note into the conversation. "In my country an optimist is a person who is studying Russian, while a pessimist is one who's studying Chinese."

There was a moment of silence and then loud laughter. The girl with the bee-hive asked her boy friend to explain. He did, saying, "He means Russian is easier to learn than Chinese." Bee-hive flashed a weak smile.

"That's not what he means," said another young man. "He means if you study Russian you believe the future world belongs to Russia, but if you study Chinese you believe it will be the Chinese who will come out on top in the end, and that this will be far worse than having the Russians running the world. True?"

"True," said I.

"Not bad," he commented, "but that would be a better story in Russia if we said an optimist is one who studies English and the pessimist the one who studies Chinese."

"You mean you'd rather be taken over by the Americans than by the Chinese?" I asked.

"Of course," he said. "We've been taken over by the Chinese before."

"It wasn't the Chinese, it was the Mongols and the Tartars," volunteered a youth named Pyotr.

"Same thing, same thing," said the Russian on my right.

"Well," I said, "this is encouraging news, but I think the day'll come when the Soviet Union and the United States will be on the same side—against the Chinese."

"Perhaps," said the owner of the derby.

Pyotr and his girl friend got up. "It's getting late," he said. "It's time for us to go home. Good night."

"What's the matter," I asked when he had gone, "is he a Komsomol?"

"Just cautious," said the derby. "I'm the Komsomol."

A wicked east wind whipped across the icy Rostov-on-Don airfield as we took off for Tiflis, the capital of Georgia. Again our transport was a much used DC-4, but this time our stewardess was the prettiest I have ever encountered on a Soviet airliner. She was in a talkative mood and brightened the early stages of the flight.

For the first one and a half hours we flew high and in gorgeous sunshine, sticking our nose into good weather just out of Rostov. Then we turned due south and the pilot kept the great Caucasian range of mountains to our left and the Black Sea to the right. We came down at Adler, the airport for Sochi, the beautiful Black Sea resort. It was like flying from Montreal to Miami in the dead of winter, for at Adler the only sign of snow was in the upper reaches of the nearby mountains.

The friendly little stewardess left the plane and her place was now taken by a real commander, a very wide-bottomed girl with passionate grey eyes. She began the flight by issuing a series of sharp orders. This did not go down well at all with the noisy Georgian passengers, who now filled all of the seats. In Georgia the male is the boss and, airplane or not, they were taking no orders from a female, and a Russian one at that.

"Stop your chatter," she shouted, facing the passengers and her back against the cabin door as if she expected us to mount a frontal attack on the captain and the crew protected behind her large and well-muscled hips. "Stop your chatter and listen to me. Come now, be orderly citizens. Put away your cigarettes. You can't smoke cigarettes on take-off and landing. Now, put away your cigarettes, and fasten your seat belts."

This was met with a roar of derisive laughter.

"I said no smoking and fasten your seat belts."

The plane was at the beginning of the runway, about to make its take-off. Not a man made a move to extinguish his cigarette or to fasten his seat belt.

"Do as I tell you," shouted the stewardess above the roar of the motors.

More laughter and loud comments in Georgian.

Down the runway scampered the plane and, leaping into the air, began a slow rise.

"If you do not follow my orders, I shall call the captain," bellowed the stewardess, her anger mounting.

More remarks in Georgian which she understood no better than I did.

Realizing the situation was hopeless, she swung open the cabin door and disappeared only to re-appear quickly with an officer in tow.

The officer was about six feet tall with broad shoulders and large hands. He stood there with an aggressive look on his face, but my fellow passengers ignored him.

"All right, then," he said in Russian. "We'll turn around, return to Adler and cancel the flight. You just see if we don't."

At that threat several of the passengers appealed to the others who now were standing or walking in the aisle. With loud protests—I supposed—in their native tongue they did sit down. But they ignored those seat belts as if they did not exist.

I silently prayed that the officer, who might be the

captain for all I knew, had not left the flying of the plane to grey-eyed big-bottom, but as the door was opened I saw the irate stewardess wildly gesticulating to a man at the controls. By now it was almost time to make a landing at nearby Sukhumi, another pleasant resort on the Black Sea.

"Fasten your seat belts, now," ordered the stewardess who had taken up her old protective position, "and those of you who don't will be handed over to the militia in Sukhumi."

A few complied, but the majority sat and stared at her and made what I presumed were rude remarks.

At Sukhumi, a few of the ringleaders of the rebellion got off, and shouting insults over their shoulders, marched off to the airport building.

Among the new passengers was a Russian of about twenty-eight, extremely handsome and dressed in a well fitting sports jacket and slacks. As soon as we were airborne, he commenced a running denunciation of the plane, its age, the condition in which it was maintained and how it smelled. He even criticized the stewardess for not sweeping the long tatty piece of carpeting that ran the length of the plane's interior. As this flood of abuse was in Russian, the stewardess handed back as much as she was getting. Finally, she suggested that if the passenger did not like the plane he should get off.

"Get off," he demanded, "where?"

"Right here in the air. I'll be glad to open the door for you."

Ignoring this invitation, he countered with, "Why was I charged so much when I happen to know that you let students ride at a cheaper rate?"

Silence from the stewardess.

"Answer me," he demanded.

She tossed her short hair and ignored him.

"I demand to know why," said Sports Suit. "I'm paying fifty per cent more than students."

"That has nothing to do with me."

We stopped briefly at Kutaisi near the Turkish frontier, and the harassed stewardess escaped further badgering by getting out of the plane and sunning herself. When we were airborne once more, the complaining passenger looked the stewardess up and down and pointed to her shoes.

"You're wearing waterproof shoes," he said.

"What of it?"

"Are you expecting rain inside the plane?"

The other passengers—all male save Tamara—whooped with laughter. The stewardess was haughty and bossy, but I felt sorry for her. As she walked beside my seat I said, "You have my sympathy."

Flashing those grey eyes, she replied, "Keep it for yourself."

The no-smoking, fasten-your-seat-belt sign lit up.

"Put away your cigarettes and fasten your seat belts."

This was greeted by another roar of laughter. Thankfully, in a few minutes we were on the ground at Tiflis, and we were met by another young woman from Intourist who introduced herself in English as Dina. From her dark looks, I correctly guessed she was Georgian. She saw that a pair of porters loaded our luggage into a waiting automobile, driven by a Georgian gentleman who must have weighed two hundred fifty pounds, and then gave the order to take us into the city.

At speeds between forty and sixty miles an hour we raced towards Tiflis down a none-too-smooth road. On the wayside I noticed one portrait of Lenin and none of Stalin. I recalled that on my last visit to Stalin's homeland this same highway had been dotted every few hundred yards with portraits of the then Soviet leader.

As the driver slowed down at the approaches to Tiflis, I was appalled by the number of shacks and decrepit houses and at the number of women sweeping the streets with long-handled brooms, the sweeping portion of which was made of twigs. At the other end of the broom was a metal gadget resembling a paint-scraper and obviously designed to clean the horse, cow and goat droppings from the paved thorough-fares.

At the Intourist Hotel on Rustaveli Prospect, Tiflis' main street, we handed over our passports for registration, were ushered into a rickety elevator operated by a middle-aged Russian woman who on that trip and every other which I made with her, either initiated or resumed an argument with the porter who happened to be on duty and was riding with her.

On the third floor, we were led to what must have been the bridal suite before the Revolution. The gigantic living-room, painted the color of old bull's blood, had two large windows overlooking the main street, a massive desk and in one corner an upright black piano which I soon learned was in tune and playable.

The ceiling of the bedroom was as lofty as that of the living-room and it too looked out on Rustaveli Prospect. It had no drapes, only a pair of lace curtains, and I saw no way whatsoever of protecting one's privacy.

The bathroom was quainter still, but although it possessed all the necessary plumbing equipment, the john was placed in the center of the room, for a reason only God and some Georgian plumber could know.

We had a deplorable lunch in the vast, windy main dining-room of this, the city's best hotel.

Years before in Georgia, I had ordered *shashlik*, one of the republic's national dishes. It was very bad *shashlik*, but time, I reasoned, might have improved the quality of the lamb and the Tiflis cooking. If possible, today's *shashlik* was worse than the other sampling, poor in quality and badly cooked and about as digestible as one of the waiter's boots. The soup was only lukewarm and the dessert un-eatable. We were visiting Tiflis out of the tourist season, of course, yet all around us Georgians and a sprinkling of Russians were eating.

Tamara, incidentally, was the only woman present; this should have tipped me off to worse things to come.

After the so-called meal, for which I paid the same Intourist price as I did at the National Hotel in Moscow, we retreated (and that is exactly what it felt like) to our suite and, after trying the piano a bit, I walked into the bedroom where Tamara was resting.

"I'm a southerner," I began.

"I know, an Alabaman."

"The Civil War broke out over a hundred years ago."

"I'll take your word for it."

"During that war a great many mistakes were made by both sides."

"*Da.*"

"But General Sherman made the biggest."

"How's that?"

"He marched through the wrong Georgia."

14. The Mountain
Road-Block

"Tiflis," begins an official guide-book for English-speaking tourists, "one of the world's oldest cities, stands on the banks of the Kura, a mountain river on the southern slopes of the Caucasian Range. The first mention of it dates back to the Fourth Century A.D., and in the Sixth Century it became the capital of Georgia.

"The history of the Georgian state is stormy and eventful, with alternating periods of prosperity and decline, aggravated by internecine struggle. Forty times Georgia was devastated by foreign invasions, and in the Eighteenth Century stood on the brink of complete subjugation by Persia and Turkey."

Next follows an amazing bit of candor. "At this dramatic moment in history, Georgia appealed for aid to its northern neighbor—Russia, and in 1801 became part of the Russian Empire." After that illuminating paragraph, the book goes on: "The overthrow of Tsarism and the establishment of the Georgian Soviet Socialist Republic inaugurated a new era in the history of the Georgian people. The economy and culture of the Georgian Republic is now developing at an unprecedented pace."

As I never had the opportunity of visiting this scenically beautiful land before the Revolution I have no means of substantiating the claims of the final paragraph, but over the last sixteen years there has been no great outward change in Tiflis. A few more apartment houses, a few more factories, a somewhat expanded school system, yes; but the housing situation was still desperate, the food bad, not many consumer items in the shops, and the standard of dress far behind Moscow, Leningrad and other Russian cities.

One of the nicest squares in Tiflis—years ago known as Liberty Square, then changed with what struck me as a clumsy piece of transition to Beria Square—was now renamed Lenin Square.

As we rode through the city behind the same large chauffeur, Dina, our shy untalkative girl guide, asked me if we had come directly from Moscow.

"No," I told her, "from Volgograd."

As she made no comment to this, I added, "You know, the former Stalingrad."

"I know, I know," she sighed.

I told her that I had attended the victory celebrations in Volgograd and that I had been surprised to hear no mention of Stalin. Dina looked at me as if she was going to burst into tears, and as the afternon drew on she became progressively gloomy.

Tiflis stands at the bottom of the impressive Mount Mtatsminda, the peak of which can only be reached by a funicular or by automobile up a long steep road with many sharp curves. As I was paying for the hire of a car, I suggested we drive to the top of the mountain for the view.

Uneasy because of the guide's and chauffeur's prolonged silence, I said for no particular reason, "So far I've seen no statues of Stalin. The last time I was in Georgia they were everywhere."

As this brought forth no reply, I asked pointedly, "Are there none left?"

"Yes. There's one in the park at the top of the mountain where we're going, and there's another at the entrance to the park down by the river."

For the remainder of the frantic journey to the summit of Mount Mtatsminda no one spoke. This was all right with me, for even on the steepest grades the chauffeur drove at a mad pace, negotiating the horseshoe curves to the accompaniment of screeching tires and grinding gears. At 6 o'clock precisely, as if we were keeping some important appointment, we reached the top of the mountain and as the driver shut off the motor there was no sound save a faint mourning of the wind through the evergreens.

The panoramic view was superb and the scenery of majestic beauty, but with every moment I became more uncomfortable. It was as if a sullen conspiracy, of which I knew not the cause, was going on about me. Six hours is an absurdly short period to form opinions about a place, but it is long enough to sense emotion and mood. I had the same feeling that I often experienced in childhood upon entering a dark and quiet forest—that at my approach a sudden hush had come over the woods, and that sinister beings that I could not identify were watching me from the dark foliage.

I got out of the car and Dina and the driver followed me, but instead of walking off with me towards the little park a hundred yards away, they remained beside the automobile. As I strolled up the path leading to the statue of Stalin—a very lonely figure on that mountain top—I had the sensation that the girl and the man were watching me. I turned around quickly but they both had their backs to me, the chauffeur looking in the direction of the distant snow-covered peaks of the surrounding mountains, and Dina's eyes seemingly set in the direction of the Georgian Military Highway, a silvery ribbon forty or more miles away. They were motionless, but I had an overpowering conviction that they had been watching me and had turned away a split second before I had stopped and looked back.

"This is silly," I said to myself and walked on in the direction of the Stalin monument. This was the first likeness of him that I had encountered since returning to the Soviet Union. I noticed that whole strips of metal lettering—which I presumed had been glowing eulogies of the man—had been removed, and not very subtly at that.

I made a few notes and walked back to the car. "If there's nothing more to be seen," I said, "then I'd appreciate it if you could drop me off at the hotel."

"There's nothing more you want to see?"

"Well, as you know, I've been to Tiflis before, and I don't have to see everything on the day of my return. Anyhow, my foot is still hurting me and I don't like to be on it too much."

"As you wish."

I thanked her and said that while in Georgia I wanted particularly to make a trip to Gori. She looked startled and asked me if she had understood me to say Gori.

"Yes, you know, Stalin's birthplace."

"I know."

"It's open to tourists, isn't it?"

"It's not on the tourist route, but I suppose you could go there. I must ask you to talk to my director about this, though. Would you like an appointment with him?"

"As soon as possible. Gori is one of the things I most want to see."

"We may be able to arrange it when we get back to the hotel."

"Thank you."

We got back into the automobile and as we began our descent to the city a carnation-colored sun was sliding down a salmon-pink sky. Behind the dark blue silhouettes of the mountains, it was a beautiful sight.

Our car had gone about a half mile, I suppose, when upon swinging around one of the dozens of really sharp curves of the desolate mountain road, I saw to my amazement up ahead what appeared to be a barricade of stones thrown up across the highway. As the road was hemmed in by high red clay banks, I sensed immediately that we were blocked. The barrier was made of hundreds of pieces of ragged-edged stones. As it had not been there when we came up the mountain, it had to be the work of several people who had erected it while I had been admiring the view from the summit of Mount Mtatsminda and re-visiting Stalin's partially mutilated statue. The wall of stones was about four feet high.

In such moments many things flash through the mind. My first thought was that this was a hold-up, and that I was carrying in my pocket several hundred dollars worth of roubles.

For a moment the driver braked, and then he changed his mind, for the car next seemed to leap through the air. As we were going downhill, quick acceleration was easy. At a speed of about fifty miles an hour he drove straight into the barricade. A loud crash and a shaking jar, and we were through the wall! As we sped away from the scene, I happened to look up to the top of the cliff on my side of the car. From behind clumps of trees I saw the faces of several men staring down on us with dark and surprised expressions.

We reached a curve and the chauffeur braked sharply to prevent our turning over, and at this dizzy height, this was a frightening prospect. I clung to the side of the vehicle as he righted the car and sped on.

Dina and the driver exchanged a flow of excited words in Georgian. I suppose I must have been thoroughly scared, because for once in my reportorial life I asked no questions. We negotiated the last few miles down the side of the mountain in complete silence. As we got out in front of the hotel—all of us behaving as if nothing had happened—I said, "I believe we are going to try to see your director?"

"Yes, will you please wait in the lobby?"

In a few minutes the meeting had been arranged, and the Intourist director, a small sandy-haired Russian in his late thirties who spoke good English, listened politely as I explained that I wanted very much to visit Gori.

"It isn't on the tourist route," he said, "but the trip can be made by car. You will have to pay extra for this, of course. When would you like to go?"

"Tomorrow."

"That will be all right. Shall we say 10 o'clock tomorrow morning? Dina will meet you here at the hotel."

"Fine. There's one thing more. My wife and I had planned to return to Moscow by train, but as I'm having trouble with my foot, I'd like to get back by plane and to move up our departure date from Tiflis."

"Of course. You must give me your travel papers and I'll see to everything. We have two planes a day from Moscow. Both are jets. I think you will like the morning one best. You take off from here, ride up in the sky for breakfast, and then when you've finished your meal, you go down and you're in Moscow."

"Sounds interesting. Let's see, this is Monday. We'll be going to Gori tomorrow. That will take all day. Could we then leave by plane for Moscow on Wednesday morning?"

"But you will be cutting short your stay with us."

"Yes, I'm afraid we will."

"All right. Leave everything to me."

I thanked him profusely, largely I believe because I had encountered no bureaucracy, and promised I would be ready to leave for Gori the following morning. I shook hands with the director, and then Dina. Without referring to the unpleasant episode on the mountainside, I made my farewells and took the elevator to my floor. The female operator was arguing with the old man in a porter's uniform. As I stepped out they were still shouting at one another.

Tamara was sorting laundry.

"I hope you'll agree," I began, "on our leaving here on Wednesday and on going back by plane."

I have never known a Muscovite in another part of the U.S.S.R. who did not want to get back to Moscow.

"Wonderful," exclaimed Tamara.

I then related what had happened on the trip to the top of Mount Mtatsminda, and the eerie feelings that overcame me while there with Dina and the silent driver.

"I think I know what's the matter," I said.

"What?"

"Stalin's haunting his homeland."

She crossed herself.

I pointed through the thin lace curtains, to the old church and the graveyard a third of the way up the mountain.

"That's where Stalin's mother is buried."

"Where?"

"Up there. In a little cemetery beside the church. I went up there the last time I was in Tiflis. I wonder if they'll move Stalin out of the Kremlin wall—"

"Beside the Kremlin wall," she corrected.

"Move him from beside the Kremlin wall to a place up there with his mother?"

She shuddered. "Let's talk about something else," she said. "These rooms—they're spooky enough as it is."

For dinner we braved the main dining-room once again. Among the one hundred or so diners, Tamara was the only woman. We sat at one of the two vacant tables and after being ignored for eight or ten minutes, I went and fetched a waiter, one who appeared to be Russian rather than Georgian.

"May we have some food?"

"Yes. Just be seated, please, and I'll come over."

Thanking him I returned to Tamara who looked not only pretty, I thought, but pretty lonely in that wasteland of Georgian males.

"They're staring at me as if I'm someone from outer space," she said.

"Let them stare."

At last the waiter arrived and asked, "What will you have?"

"First of all a menu, if you don't mind."

He disappeared and it was another four or five minutes before he returned, but he did have a bill of fare—of sorts.

"At lunch," I began, "we tried the *shashlik*, and it was, well——"

"I know," he said, "you don't have to tell me. It was no good."

"Can't we get *shashlik* in Tiflis?"

"We have difficulty in getting the meat."

"Then could we have steaks?"

"You can try," was his hardly encouraging reply.

"In the meantime, will you bring me a bottle of good red wine, please?"

"With pleasure."

The wine came and it was excellent.

While we were awaiting the steaks, a tall, well-dressed man with the close-cropped mustache much favored in this part of the world, got up from the table where he had been sitting with three other men and lurched over to our table.

"How dare you bring a nice young woman into a place like this?" he demanded in heavily-accented Russian.

I told him my wife and I were staying at the hotel and this was the only place I knew to bring her for a meal.

"In Georgia," he hissed, "we leave our women at home."

"Don't worry," I said, "the next time I'm going to leave my woman at home—and it's going to be a long way from here. In the meantime, I'd appreciate it if you would go away."

He grasped one of the empty chairs at our table and braced himself.

"Do me a big favor," I said, "and go away."

Muttering something unpleasant about Russians, he staggered off.

"Look," I said, "a woman."

Accompanied by a tie-less but otherwise well-dressed

man of about forty, a dark-eyed, dark-haired pretty woman, who despite her brunette looks did not appear to be Georgian, entered the room.

By this time all the tables were occupied. After studying the room for some time, and staring at us for a moment or two, they sat at a table with a pair of men. The couple had hardly had time to summon a waiter, when one of the men they had joined stretched his arms before him on the table, lowered his head and went to sleep. The man and woman rose and hurriedly left the restaurant.

"Promise me one thing," said Tamara. "If anything happens, don't hit anyone."

"No fear. I have no desire to be jailed, especially in Tiflis."

At last the waiter brought our meal and with it a large plate of that excellent hot Georgian bread featured by the Aragvai restaurant in Moscow.

When I asked the waiter why there were no women present, he explained that before the Soviet regime women never appeared in a public restaurant in Georgia, but that nowadays a few came in. "Not many, though," he added.

Never had I seen so much wine consumed. Waiters were constantly delivering six or so bottles to a table and—I thought it odd—seldom removing them, which made for very crowded tables.

Midway through the steak—which was better than we imagined it would be—the man with the open-necked shirt re-appeared with his pretty companion and made for our table.

"May we sit here?" he asked.

Delighted to have company, I said we would be most pleased.

"Foreigners?" asked the man.

"Yes, Americans."

"Ah," he said. His date said nothing.

In her perfect Russian, Tamara asked the woman if

what the waiter had told us was true, that few women frequented the restaurant.

"I don't know," she replied. "I'm Ukrainian."

The man confirmed what the waiter had told us. As our new companions consulted the menu, Tamara and I conversed about small matters and asked for another bottle of wine. "And take away this bottle," I said, indicating the empty. When he hesitated I picked it up and handed it to him.

With a smile, my tablemate explained that it was the custom to leave the bottles on the table, for in that way the waiter could determine how many had been consumed.

"Well," I said, "if he can add one and one, he won't have any trouble with us."

As the wine flowed and our companions limbered up conversationally, I asked the man if bringing my wife into the restaurant was the reason why I had been receiving so many hostile stares.

"That and the fact they think you're Russian," he answered.

"You mean they don't like Russians?"

"Some people don't."

"Why is that?"

He shrugged his shoulders. I saw that he did not want to talk about this, but I am afraid I pressed him.

"Is it because of Stalin?"

"It's possible."

"But why? Don't you agree that he was, well, that he did a lot of harm to a lot of people?"

"He may have been a rascal, but he was one of ours. He came from here, you know, but excuse me, I must talk to my companion." I knew that he knew I was being boorish.

"Forgive me," I told him.

"That's all right. I know it's hard to understand."

"Really it's not. In America we've got an old saying, 'He may be a bastard but he's our bastard.' "

He smiled and said nothing.

The Ukrainian lady had ordered roast chicken and, when it was served, she asked the waiter for pepper. He replied that the restaurant had none. "We haven't had pepper for years," he said.

At this juncture a group of musicians walked on to the bandstand, and like their counterparts in Rostov-on-Don, opened up full blast. As we were sitting fairly close, conversation became impossible, but as the evening wore on the volume diminished. The diners ignored the musicians and under the circumstances and in this strange place, Tamara and I decided we could forego dancing. Our friends took the same view, and there was no dancing.

The leader of the band was a violinist who had had his fiddle amplified, and he accounted for a lot of noise. When he and the trumpeter played along together, the din was awful. After a while the violinist slapped a mute on his instrument and things were better, and when the horn man decided to leave the stand, conversation again became possible.

"I like your suit," said the man. "Did you have it made in America?"

"We live in England. I had it made there."

I complimented him on his sports jacket.

"My brother made it. He's a master tailor."

"Do you think anyone would mind if I smoked?" asked Tamara.

The man advised against it. "Our women seldom smoke," he said, "and never in public."

As it was now late, I asked my wife if she was ready to go and she said that as pleasant as was our company she did feel we had better say good night. With this I told our companions how much we had enjoyed their company, paid the waiter and prepared to depart.

"You asked about Stalin," said the man after the well-tipped waiter moved away. "May I just say, speaking as a Georgian, to do what they have done to him is wrong. One day he will be regarded by the whole world as a great man."

"But his purges and all that—"

"I know. I know. But you have to treat some people that way."

"I'm sorry, but what people should be treated as Stalin treated them? He robbed man of his dignity."

He lifted his shoulders, sighed, shook hands with me again and bid us good night. I had been dismissed—as a fool or a misunderstanding foreigner, or both.

At the door an aged and shriveled drunk came up to me and in worse Russian than mine, said, "Why don't you go back to Moscow? You're not welcome here."

"I'm not a Russian."

He said something in Russian and staggered off.

"From now on," I told Tamara, "we're eating all our meals in our room."

15. Joseph Stalin's Birthplace

In the mountain village of Gori, on December 21, 1879, a male child was born to Catherine and Vissarion Djugashvili and they called him Joseph. Later in life, Joseph Djugashvili called himself Joseph Stalin, meaning man of steel.

As a child, he was far from pretty. He was small, sallow and sickly and before he was ten he contracted smallpox which left his face pitted with pockmarks. He was born with no separation between two toes on his left foot, and his left arm was stiff and shorter than his right. There are several versions as to how this came about. Stalin said he injured his arm and this led to infection and then blood-poisoning, but members of his family have been quoted as saying Stalin's arm was malformed at birth.

He was not an outstanding pupil. By his own admission it took him six years to graduate from a four year institution, but this could have been because of his numerous illnesses.

On a previous visit to Gori, I met an old man who told me his uncle had been one of Stalin's teachers. When I asked about the standard of the boy's scholarship, the old man peered about to make sure no one could hear him as he whispered, "My uncle always maintained he was a poor student and an insolent one. He was always getting into fights and he was usually beaten, but no one could ever accuse him of cowardice. One of his troubles was taunting boys who were bigger and stronger than he was."

Stalin's mother was a devout Christian and she prayed that her son would become a priest. His studies at Gori were at a religious preparatory school. From there he went to the Greek Orthodox Theological Seminary in Tiflis, and it was there that he first heard of Karl Marx, not in his regular lessons, of course, but in clandestine sessions with forbidden books. He fell in love with the inventor of what is known as Communism and it was a life-long affection. In later years, Stalin's interpretation of Marx's doctrine probably would have repelled the author of *Das Kapital*.

With each month at the seminary—which appears to have been more of a hot-bed of rebellion than a religious institution—Stalin became more arrogant and unruly. At last the authorities became exasperated and expelled him.

Stalin did not return to Gori. He remained in Tiflis, leading a thoroughly disorganized personal life, sleeping in hovels and doing part-time work where he could find it, one job being at the Tiflis Observatory. In those days, he was scruffy and unwashed, a non-conformist in most matters and it is no exaggeration to say he was an early Georgian beatnik.

As he became the dictator of the Soviet Union and of millions of people in the countries of eastern Europe, he was all but deified in his old home-town. A marble shrine was built around the two-roomed wooden hut that was said to have been his birthplace. Thousands of people came from all over the U.S.S.R. to stand in awe before the hut and gaze at its primitive interior, with its crude bed, chairs, table and framed pictures of Stalin and his mother. There was also a picture of Lenin, who looked truly out of company. Near the shrine had been erected a Stalin Museum, and the whole building was enclosed by a stone and steel wall, which was singularly appropriate.

With the nationwide de-Stalinization, what had happened at Gori? I wanted to know and see, and I was thankful that the trip there by car had been so easily arranged by Intourist.

On the day of my journey to Stalin's birthplace, Tamara awakened with a terrible cold. As she also felt feverish, she asked for a thermometer and a packet of aspirin (in Russian pronounced aus-p'-RIN). I was reasonably sure that these articles could be more readily obtained by Intourist than by me and accordingly made this request. Dina was tremendously solicitous about my wife's welfare and volunteered to get the thermometer and medicine before we set out for Gori. The thermometer must have caused difficulty, because forty-five minutes went by before Dina, breathlessly apologetic for the delay, arrived at our rooms with medicine and thermometer. Yes, Tamara had a fever, but after medicating herself with the aspirin, she assured me she would be all right alone in Tiflis while I made my pilgrimage to Gori.

Before Khrushchev's denunciation of Stalin at the Twentieth Congress of the Communist Party in 1956, the undulating, twisting highway from Tiflis to Gori was peppered with roadside full-length statues and busts of the old Georgian.

After Dina, the driver and I had travelled about twelve of the sixty-five miles to Gori—without sighting a single likeness or even reference to Stalin, I turned to my guide and remarked on how things had changed.

"Yes," said Dina, "all the statues have gone but one. There's one left in Mtskheta."

"That's the old capital of Georgia, isn't it?"

"Yes."

"You know, this road once had thirty or forty statues of Stalin."

"Yes."

"And now there's just the one?"

"Yes."

"What did they do with the others?"

"I don't know."

"Who removed them?"

"I don't know."

Dina took a handkerchief from her bag and applied it first to her nose and then to her eyes.

"My God," I said to myself, "is she going to weep?"

The ride between Tiflis and Gori contains some magnificent scenery. In many places the road runs alongside the swift-flowing river Kura and often beneath dark towering cliffs atop which stand the ruins of ancient fortresses and castles. In silence and with Dina still swabbing at eyes and nose, we swept through the outskirts of Mtskheta, until the sixth century the capital of Georgia.

"Tell him to slow down, please," I asked.

We rolled past the Samtavr Nunnery, dedicated to Nina, an early Georgian queen, the Sveti Tskkoveli Cathedral, and the restored Samtavr temple.

"Would you like to stop here?" asked the guide.

"No, thank you. I have seen them all before. Where is the Stalin statue?"

"Just up the road."

"Will you please have the driver stop when we come to it?"

She looked at me and nodded.

It was there all right, just beside the road, a full-length replica of the Generalissimo in a long military overcoat and military cap, but there was a great difference since I had last seen this statue. The bronze plaques with their profuse eulogies of the Soviet leader had been torn from the base of the monument. Not that any was needed, yet there was not a single identification of the man.

As I was looking it over, a middle-aged man and woman came along the road. We nodded to one another.

"No matter what you think," said the man in Russian, "that was a great person."

"Thank you for speaking up," I said. "I'm an American, a correspondent. I have been hearing that you Georgians are now paying for Stalin's sin."

He said something to the woman in Georgian and she walked away. Lowering his voice, he said, "In a way that's true. While life gets better for people in other parts of the country, we are neglected."

I heard footsteps behind me.

"Good-bye," said the man, moving off quickly.

I turned around and saw our driver. He pointed to his watch.

"Should we be leaving?" I asked.

He nodded his head.

From Mtskheta to Gori, a grape-growing part of Georgia, large numbers of men and women were busy doing to grapevines whatever has to be done to them before spring. It was a change from post-war days to see that the ratio between men and women workers was about equal. Just after the war the women in the fields outnumbered the men by about nine to one. A fierce, brave and warlike people, the Georgians lost heavily in World War II.

At the approaches to Gori two things were missing—the prison, or detention center of some sort, that used to stand on the right of the road as you entered the town, and a large white statue of Stalin on the left of the highway.

The place of imprisonment, with its barbed wire fences and goon boxes—with the prisoners in full view—had completely disappeared and given way to open fields. Where Stalin's statue once stood, there was a replica of what appeared to be a huge stag at bay. We drove straight on to the shrine.

When we got there, I could find no changes. There was the same furniture, the same photographs. Even Lenin's photo was still hanging in the same spot.

There were changes inside the museum, however. Gone

were the framed quotations from the writings of that other
Georgian, L. P. Beria. The excessive gushings of other
Kremlin leaders on the subject of their then beloved leader
were also missing, but the report cards from Stalin's school-
days, letters to his daughter Svetlana, strangely gentle and
fatherly, and the chart showing Stalin's escape routes from
his various banishments to Siberia under the last Tsar—all
were still to be seen.

I said that it seemed odd that we were the only visitors.

"It's because this is a closed day," said Dina.

"But the gates are open and there's nothing to stop anyone from visiting the shrine."

There was no comment.

"Well," said I, "we might as well head back."

"Have you seen enough?"

"Yes. I wanted to see what, if any, changes had been
made here."

"There are no changes."

"I'm sorry to differ with you, but a lot of those slogans
about Stalin have been removed from the museum."

"What slogans? I don't know what you are talking
about."

"Slogans, or quotations, or whatever you want to call
them, that praised Stalin as the leader and teacher of the
Soviet people, as the wisest and greatest of all men."

Dina sniffed into her handkerchief and made no comment.
As we left Gori, she became more silent and withdrawn than
ever. We had gone about ten miles, I suppose, when she
suddenly cried out something in Georgian, threw open the
window on her side of the car and gasped for air. The driver
brought the car to a quick stop. Poor Dina was sick all over
the place.

I offered her my large handkerchief and comforted her
as best I could.

"I'm all right now," she said, "and thank you."

She told the chauffeur to go on.

"I'm terribly sorry," she said just above a whisper.

"Forget it," I replied, "and see here, you mustn't get depressed like this. You mustn't let all this business about Stalin affect you so much, so personally—"

She looked stunned.

"I'm not depressed or sad. I just suffer terribly from car sickness."

"You know," I told her, "when I was first starting out in the newspaper business, my editor called me to his desk one day and told me that the big state prison had been experiencing one riot after another. 'I want you to go out there and talk to the warden and find out the trouble, Gilmore,' he said. 'Yes, sir,' I said taking off.

"The warden was nice and patient with me. I asked him about the food, the prison discipline, what was being done to rehabilitate the men, and so on. Finally, the warden turned to me and said, 'Hell, son, it ain't anything like that. Them men just want *out!*'"

Dina smiled faintly.

"It's a little like that with you. All this time, ever since we met, I've been thinking you were terribly depressed over the denigration of Stalin. Now I discover you've been car sick all the time. Hell, you just want *out.*"

From then on Dina and I were friends.

Back at the hotel in Tiflis I found Tamara much better, and with a normal temperature. As I had eaten no lunch, and as she had skipped hers, we decided on an early dinner— in our rooms.

We were served by an acrobatic, friendly and attentive Georgian waiter who assured me that most guests, especially if they were with ladies, ate in their rooms. After our experiences in the main dining-room below, we could understand why.

In serving us the waiter made at least six round trips to the kitchen, bounding in and out of the room, balancing a tray above his head with his right hand. He kept his left hand extended, and waved it backward and forward as if his hand were a sword that he was using to slash his way through a dense crowd.

On each appearance he would compliment Tamara on how well she spoke Russian. "But," he asked, "do you know Georgian wine? You have to know more than a knowledge of Russian to understand wine."

Anticipating him, Tamara asked, "What wine do you recommend?"

"A white wine, number 12."

"Fine," said I, "a bottle of number 12."

This turned out to be amber-colored and of excellent taste. So excellent, in fact, that we ordered a second bottle. In the great gloom of our cavernous living-room, the good cool wine raised our flagging spirits. Because of the dismal illumination from a pair of forty-watt bulbs, the walls, the ceiling and even the floor were a mass of shadows through which a variety of grotesque and frightening shapes seemed to appear and disappear.

At precisely six o'clock, the street outside our windows echoed with a wild cacophony of bird-twittering. On previous nights I had ignored the noise, but on this occasion I got up to witness a very strange sight. Thousands upon thousands of starlings were streaking past our windows, all hell bent in the same direction. They looked like countless blobs of dirty snow being driven by a terrific gale. In the space of a few minutes the limbs of the sycamore trees that line Rustaveli Prospect were completely covered. Twittering and shrieking, the starlings fought for roosting positions along the bare branches that sagged until I thought they would break.

Turning to Tamara I asked, "Do you mind if I make an obvious comment?"

"Go on, you usually do."

"I can sum up the Intourist Hotel in Tiflis in five short words."

"What are they?"

"A hotel for the birds."

"You'd better have some more wine. This place is getting on your nerves."

The waiter made another sweep into the room and skated around the table at a forty-five degree angle.

"Slow down," I called out. "I want to ask you something."

"Yes, *gospodin?*"

"Where do all those birds come from?"

"I don't know, but they always appear at just this time. You can set your watch by them."

Out of the room he flew.

"How can that be?" asked my wife. "It's getting lighter every evening. Surely those birds must time themselves by sunset, not his watch."

"Don't be so factual."

As the birds settled down for the night, they lowered their noise by about a half million decibels and made a noise that now sounded like water in the rapids of a swiftly-flowing, narrow river. Another horrific touch was the lighting from outside. The street illuminations were yellow and cast an eerie light up through the trees and into the upper reaches of the windows.

The furniture of our suite can best be described as late Soviet—which is better than early Soviet. The wardrobe was made of heavily grained light wood liberally dotted with knots. "Just study it in this light and the shadows," said Tamara. "Now what do you see?" I looked at it for a moment and through the gloom there appeared the pugnacious mug of a large bulldog.

"Bulldog," I exclaimed.

"Exactly. Now look up there in the corner. What do you see?"

"I'm afraid to say. Here, let's finish this wine. We've got to get to bed. The car's coming for us early tomorrow morning."

"How early must we get up?"

"Oh, about 5:30."

"God of mine, but that's all right. We'll be getting back to Moscow so it doesn't matter."

"You mean we'll be getting out of here."

Fortunately we slept soundly and my portable alarm clock went off before the birds did.

Leaving our packed bags in the room we walked down the two flights of broad carpeted stairs to the half darkness of the lobby. The elevator with the perpetually angry lady operator was not working at this early hour, but we could not have used it at a later hour either. There was no call button on our landing, and on my earlier inquiry about this, I was told that the elevator was for the use of passengers ascending, but not for descending.

At six o'clock in the morning the lobby resembled the Moscow Art Theatre setting for Maxim Gorky's *The Lower Depths*. A porter in an old army overcoat that touched the ground mutely consented to go fetch our bags, and when he returned with them he only grunted when I tipped him the equivalent of one dollar.

After a few minutes of waiting we were met by Dina and left for the airport—in deep despair, I should add—for the forecast from Moscow on my portable radio the night before had predicted fog in the capital. From long experience of being grounded at airstrips all over the U.S.S.R., I was certain that our journey to the Tiflis Airport would be a dry run and conclude with a return to our spooky hotel suite.

At this hour, it was still quite dark in Tiflis and the airport was packed with would-be passengers, many of them asleep in their seats or on the floor. Dina located two empty seats in a side room and told us to sit there while she registered our tickets. Next to me was a swarthy young Georgian in very narrow cuffless trousers. A guitar was suspended from his shoulders by a blue ribbon.

At 7:15 an announcement over the loud speakers, first in Georgian and then in Russian, said the Moscow plane would be taking off shortly, and ordered all ticket-holders to board their plane. In the midst of a shoving loud-talking mob, we were led through a barrier where we said our farewells to Dina. Someone pushed us towards a huge Tupolev 102 jet and we were escorted to two seats, between a pair of windows. We looked out on nothing but the wall of the airliner. I noticed that the only other obvious foreigner among the horde of passengers—a young Englishman— was also placed at a seat with no window and I could not help but wonder if we had been purposely placed where we could see nothing more than the inside of the plane.

As unruly as ever, the Georgians—all males—marched about the plane when they were supposed to be seated, and even as the plane roared into the air some of them were still on their feet. From what I had observed, Georgians disdain fastening their seat-belts and obviously regard it as cowardice.

Breakfast was lukewarm tea, spiced sausage, a sweet cake and an orange. To my consternation I learned that the whole crew, from the stewardesses to the captain, was Georgian. Nevertheless, it was a splendid trip into Moscow's Vnukova Airport. It was from this airport that I had finally got out of Moscow with my family ten years previously. I remembered vividly the faces of the friends from many embassies who turned out to say good-bye. At the last moment, the Second Secretary of the Italian Embassy, Elio Pascarelli, the accordionist of The Kremlin Krows, dashed across the airfield to hammer on the sides of the DC-4 that was taking us to Helsinki, until an irate stewardess opened the door. With that, Pascarelli climbed aboard and flinging his arms first around Tamara and then me, gave us a good Neapolitan farewell.

Instead of the predicted fog, Moscow was ablaze with sunshine. I had sent a telegram from Tiflis asking Intourist to meet me with a car, as by contract they were supposed to do. Something had gone wrong and there was no Intourist representatives and no car. We took a taxi.

Back at the National we were warmly welcomed, almost as if we had come home.

"Winter's gone, *gospodin*," called out the doorman. "It's spring again."

The sky was light blue and cloudless. The snow was melting fast and outside our fifth floor window, a pair of pigeons was making love.

As we had a dinner date that evening, Tamara rested. The weather was so perfect and my ailing foot so much better, that I decided to take a walk in Red Square just as I had done on my first evening in Moscow twenty-two years before.

Strolling past the spot where once stood the Shrine of the Iberian Virgin, I looked up at the pink wall of the V. I. Lenin Museum where for years a plaque proclaimed: "RELIGION IS OPIUM FOR THE PEOPLE." But it had disappeared.

I walked into Red Square to view again one of my favorite sights—the magnificent Church of St. Basil the Blessed, with its sugarplum and onion turrets. Then on I went to stand before the Mausoleum from which Joseph Stalin's body had been banished, and which now contained only the embalmed body of Lenin. When I left Moscow in 1953, there were two names above the doorway, LENIN-STALIN. Today there was only the one, LENIN.

A full moon hung in the brilliant afternoon sky and its faint light seemed to fuse with the sun's in sparkles on the red stars atop the Kremlin towers. I stood there looking at the concrete reviewing stands beside Lenin's tomb, stands from which I had witnessed so many May Day and November the Seventh parades, and listened to so many speeches. As memories flooded over me and the good and bad times of twelve years in Moscow unrolled before my inner eye in the jerky sequences of an early movie, one face stood out from all the rest—that of Tamara. Moscow did many things to me, but it gave me her, a very precious thing to receive from any city.

16. Two Siberians and the Great Chinese Divide

"Mahdom needs fattening up," exclaimed Luba the chambermaid as we dressed for dinner.

"Fattening up?" said Tamara. "I've just been saying to myself that I must go on a diet."

"No, no, Mahdom. You're too skinny as it is. If you lose any more weight, your husband will be able to see through you like a glass of water."

"No fear."

"*Gospodin*, you should feed her more."

"Luba?"

"*Gospodin?*"

"Tell me, in the eyes of a Russian man, what sort of figure should the perfect woman have?"

"That's easy. The sort of woman he can slap on the bottom when he leaves for work in the morning, and—"

"Go on."

"Forgive me, Mahdom and *gospodin*."

"Of course."

"Ideally," she added with a laugh, "his wife's slapped bottom should still be shaking when he returns home in the evening. Now, that's a real woman. She's soft and jolly and good tempered and as warm in winter as a Dutch oven."

It was almost ten when we entered the restaurant for dinner. The place was packed with diners and dancers, but the headwaiter found us places at a table where two men were sitting together, and apparently not greatly enjoying themselves.

"Would you mind if this American gentleman and his lady joined you?"

Surprisingly, they both got to their feet and the elder of the two, whom I shall call Konstantin, a dark haired, broad shouldered man of about forty-five, made an old fashioned and charming low bow. The younger, who shall be Ilya, bobbed his head and smiled. In two or three minutes we learned they were Siberians on a business trip to Moscow.

"Siberia, now that's the place for you," began Konstantin, "that's the land of the future. We have great cities growing up there that will one day outshine Moscow and Leningrad. Have you ever been to my country?"

"Yes, but it was a long time ago," I told him.

"How much of the country did you see?"

"A great deal of it. I flew from Moscow, straight across Siberia, making several stops."

"And then you flew back to Moscow?"

"No I didn't. I flew a very great distance. I flew up to Yakutsk, and then over the Bering Strait into Alaska."

"My God, I'm a Siberian and I've never been to Yakutsk. But have you ever been to Verkhoyansk, the coldest place in the world? The average temperature in January is 59 degrees below zero Fahrenheit, and I've known it to go down to 90 below."

"No, I didn't get to Verkhoyansk, and if you'll forgive me, I'm not going there."

"Siberia's like the great West in America," said Konstantin. "We've got everything out there, just as your West has everything. We've got cattle, oil, coal, gold, diamonds—"

"You don't have Texas millionaires," I interrupted.

"And you don't have Neiman-Marcus," said Tamara.

"What's that?"

"It's a store. Like GUM."

"We've got a GUM in Siberia. Lots of them."

"What about Siberian millionaires?"

"We have collective farms that are millionaires."

"Not the same as a Texas millionaire," I said.

"I don't suppose so. But we'll have them one of these days."

"Under Communism?"

"Who knows?" He roared with laughter. "Here's a toast. To Siberian millionaires."

I was enjoying this man tremendously.

"How do you know about the West?" I asked.

"I've been there, Tovarich. I've been to Texas, to Oklahoma, the whole thing—Arizona and New Mexico too. Now, Texas, that's a state for you. I loved it. It's so much like Siberia—cotton, cattle, waving fields of grain, and the Mexicans."

"Well, that's a difference. You don't have any Mexicans in Siberia."

"Oh, don't we now?" He dropped his voice to look around him. "We've got the Chinese. They're our Mexicans."

I whooped with delight.

"Not so funny if you're a Siberian."

"Not at all," chimed in the younger man, Ilya. "Do you know that we live alongside millions of Chinese, with the longest frontier in the world?"

"Of course he knows that." This from Konstantin.

"But we share a long frontier with Canada," I told them.

"Canadians are not Chinese," said the older man, as he laughed and banged the table.

"I'll certainly agree with you there. But let me see if I understand you. Are you implying that you'd be happier living alongside Canadians than Chinese?"

"How many Canadians are there?"

"Oh, ten or eleven million, I suppose."

"There you are," said Konstantin. "There're six or seven hundred million Chinese."

"But they're your friends."

"That's what the politicians tell us."

"The people in Moscow and this part of the Soviet Union are always worrying about the Germans," said Ilya, "and, of course, I'm not saying anything's wrong with that because they've had plenty of trouble from the Germans, but out in Siberia we know that we've been invaded, I mean our country's been invaded—"

"I know," I spoke up. "You've been invaded far more successfully from the East than from the West. I've heard that before."

"It's true."

"I'm not disagreeing."

I asked them their opinion of the rift between the U.S.S.R. and the Chinese Communists.

"Let's leave that to the politicians," said Konstantin, and he said it rather firmly. "I think we've talked enough about the Chinese. What about this music? What is the orchestra playing?"

"*Podmoskovnie Vechera*," said Ilya.

"It's the best tune I've heard in the Soviet Union for many years," I said.

"I don't care much for this place." This from Konstantin.

"What's the matter with it?"

"The orchestra plays too softly and the lights are too low. I like a loud band and bright lights, so you can hear what you're dancing to and see the girls and what they're wearing."

I looked the dancers over. It was the prettiest and best dressed group of girls I had seen in Moscow.

The smarter dressed ones seemed to use little lipstick, and lots of eye-shadow and makeup. They wore well cut sweaters and silk skirts and one or two couples danced cheek-to-cheek.

I asked Konstantin what he thought of that.

"Why not?" he smiled.

At that Ilya asked Tamara for a dance.

To Konstantin I remarked that his friend didn't dance cheek-to-cheek.

"He wouldn't dare," he replied, "she's a lady and your wife."

At the end of the evening—which I counted as an amusing one—Konstantin said to Tamara, "I heard you say one of your daughters collects match boxes. Here, please take her this one. It's from Siberia. And don't forget Siberia. It's the land of the future."

"Even with those Chinese?"

He frowned.

"I'm sorry," I said, "but I hope you'll forgive me for this is a fascinating problem."

He lowered his head. "Not fascinating if you have to live alongside them."

"What's going to be the answer?"

"Once upon a time," he said with a broad smile, "I imagine they asked that question in Texas."

He extended his hand and gave mine a firm handshake.

"Come to Siberia, my friends, and now good night."

The Soviet-Chinese dispute—which in late 1963 and early 1964 reached a state of shrill and almost hysterical acerbity—is one of the most fantastic international wrangles of the century. If allowed to continue in its present intensity, it could have a profound effect upon us all, our children and our children's children. It is astounding that the leaders of the two Communist countries have allowed their quarrel to reach the stage that it has. And this raises the question—is there really any way they can settle it?

Short of the death, disability, or fall from power of either Nikita S. Khrushchev or Mao Tse-tung, no quick and lasting solution seems possible. There are, in fact, good reasons for believing that the controversy will become even more bitter, and relations between Moscow and Peking immeasurably worse.

The deadly humorless propaganda machines of both Communist Parties weekly grind out new charges and fresh insults against one another, while the chieftains of each nation make accusatory and uncomplimentary off-the-record asides about their counterparts. But what about the people?

I am unable to report on the Chinese because I have not talked to them, but I have talked with many Russians on the subject of the great divide. Already I have related several instances of their reaction to, and their awareness of, the Chinese problem. When you raise the subject with Russians —and I am not talking about officials—you seldom fail to receive a lively response, but I must emphasize that the average Soviet citizen is not very greatly worked up over his government's row with Peking.

During and after the last war, I was time and again dumbfounded by the lack of interest in world issues, or even matters of vital internal importance, shown by the average Russian man and woman. Knowing in advance that some momentous announcement was to be made at a certain time by Moscow Radio, I have sat in Russian homes and excitedly awaited the reaction of Russian friends and acquaintances as the news rolled from their radios and home loud speakers. Over and over again, I have seen these ordinary Soviet citizens listen politely and then, with not so much as an exclamation or serious comment, return to a discussion of the intimate affairs of family life, or the mundane problems of their own day-to-day life.

I once asked a Russian friend about this apparent indifference to important political news and he replied, "It's not indifference. We are weary and bored and disillusioned with politics and can anyone blame us?"

I asked him to go on.

"All right. I grew up reading and listening to speeches by our leaders condemning Hitler and his gang. I heard about it at my school and over the radio when I came home in the evening. It was drummed into me at Young Pioneer meetings, and as I grew older, by the Komsomols. Then, overnight, I was told that my country had made a pact with Hitler and all the evil men who surrounded him and performed such acts of terror on the Jews and others. No explanation was given to us why this was done, why all of a sudden these terrible people had become bound to us by a pact. I can tell you I was more than a little confused."

He ran his hand through his hair and smiled.

"Then these new friends of ours attacked us, and we were told all over again what fascist hyenas they were, and once again no one made any explanations. Yet you must remember that before our country was invaded by the Germans, up to a very few months before Hitler launched his attack on us, the Second World War was the imperialists' war. Then all this changed. Once we were attacked, it was a just war and we were asked to fight for the great Soviet Fatherland. Of course this was later changed to an appeal to defend the great Russian Motherland."

This man, as close a Russian friend as I ever had, put his hand on my knee and said, "And then there was the case of you Americans. As a young boy I was taught you were a nation of blood-sucking capitalists. What happens? You become our allies and you send us all sorts of aid, food, jeeps, and whole factories and thousands of trucks. I'll admit that our government and our Party never thanked you very warmly, but they appreciated it and so did the Russian people."

He said all this without anger or bitterness and, of course, it made sense.

"But the greatest confusion of all was yet to come," he continued. "I refer to Stalin. I am a child of the Revolution and from the days of my earliest recollection I remember him as a Man-God, the wisest, kindest, most all-seeing human being there was, in my country or any other, Stalin the infallible, our leader and teacher. If we had Stalin we didn't need a God. Then one day he's dead and people dare to whisper that life is better without him, and finally our new leader smashes to pieces the Man-God of my youth and he is a monster. I don't know if you people in the West will ever realize the psychological effect of the denunciation of Stalin on the Russian people."

He laughed and shook his head.

"So now what have we got?" he continued. "They've done a backflip on our Chinese Communist brothers. For years we've read and listened to their praise. And now, well, they're almost as bad as you Americans. No, I'm sorry, but I pay very little attention to the propaganda."

"What about The Voice of America and Radio Free Europe?" I asked.

"Excuse me, but I pay very little attention to anyone's propaganda, yours or ours, and I think this goes for a great many Russian people."

"But the lights are burning long and bright in the Kremlin every night as your leaders wrestle with the Chinese problem," I said.

"Well, let them. That's their job, I suppose. As for me, I've got other things to worry about than the Chinese."

"Such as what?"

"Such as that new apartment I've been promised and, when the time comes, who's going to win the football championship next summer."

Up until the death of Stalin, the men in the Kremlin were completely contemptuous of Soviet public opinion, what little of it that existed. They could turn it off and on like a hot and cold faucet, but things are different now. A more informed public opinion is slowly gathering shape and the people are no longer content to follow without question or reservation the dizzy zig-zags and unexplained contradictions of the Communist Party line. Even my friend's indifference to propaganda is, in itself, opinion.

In their attitudes and relations towards the West, Mr. Khrushchev and his associates have made some glaring propaganda errors, but they are making very few in their great disagreement with the Chinese. The Russians have come down hard on the racial issue, accusing Peking of wanting to set the colored peoples of the world against the whites. For home consumption the Soviet propagandists know what they are doing, for no matter how loudly they disclaim it, the Soviets—or to be more specific, the Russian people—do have a color prejudice. There have been numerous and lamentable cases of discrimination against African students in Moscow in recent years.

I recall at least four cases of American-born Negroes who became Soviet citizens—and regretted it. They came to my home or my office (and at the time they did it, this took some courage) and poured out their complaints against discrimination. During the last months of World War II, when Soviet and Japanese relations were in an extremely delicate stage and both Governments were doing a great deal towards not provoking the other, I was present when a Soviet General (he is now a Marshal) shook his fist in the faces of a pair of Japanese correspondents and actually called them "yellow devils!" To many Russians there is not a big difference between a Chinese and a Japanese. They both have differently colored skins than the Slav, both speak a foreign language, and eat different food than he does.

In the years before the Soviet-Chinese split, when the seven hundred million yellow people beyond the U.S.S.R.'s frontier were being revered as the Russians' closest friends and brothers, Soviet students at Moscow University became disenchanted with their Peking colleagues. They particularly resented their pedantic and grim attitude towards university life and an overall outlook that seemed priggish in the extreme. The spartan philosophy of eating rice and sleeping in the shop has no appeal to Russians.

My wife has many cousins. Several of them are recent graduates of Moscow University. Discussing Chinese students one of them said to me, "They're not human, I tell you. They study too much and they take everything too seriously. They are clannish and they don't like to mix. I can't imagine getting to be a good friend with a Chinese."

"What about the Chinese girl students?" I asked.

"I only knew one," he said, "and she was enough. At a party one evening I began flirting with her. Why, she turned on me as if I were about to tear down the Great Wall of China to seduce the Chinese state. Oh, no! No Chinese friends for me. I prefer the Americans, the English, the French and the Italians."

When current Soviet propaganda hammers away on the subject of pigmentation politics, they are beating a drum that will command attention from its own people—if no other. There is a Chinese saying, "When the dragon whispers, men's shouts are drowned."

In late September, 1963, Peking's Party newspaper, *People's Daily*, said: "If his memory is not too short, Khrushchev should, of course, remember that during the period of Stalin's leadership he (Khrushchev) himself was particularly active in supporting the then prevailing policy of suppressing counter-revolutionaries."

The newspaper recalled that during the purges of the late 1930's, Khrushchev joined in the loud baying for the lives of the accused saying: "In lifting their hands against Comrade Stalin they lifted their hands against all of us, the working class and the working people." Mr. Khrushchev is extremely sensitive to criticism, and ultra-sensitive on the subject of his long and blind subservience to Stalin. On several occasions he has flown into a towering rage when reminded of it, and he has yet to make a satisfactory explanation of his record during the dictatorship of his late boss.

The Chinese have also accused Khrushchev of attacking

Stalin as "a pretext for interfering in the internal affairs of the fraternal Communist Parties of other countries"—a most heinous crime. *People's Daily* said: "Khrushchev has maligned Stalin as a murderer. Does this not mean that the International Communist movement had a murderer as its teacher for decades? If Stalin was an idiot, as Khrushchev says he was, does this not mean that the great Soviet Army, which triumphed in the anti-fascist war, had an idiot as its supreme commander?

"Stalin made mistakes," the paper went on, "but his merits outweighed his faults, and the great majority of the Soviet people disapprove of such abuse of Stalin." The article ended with this gratuitous advice to Stalin's successor: "We hope you will become aware of your errors and return from your wrong path to the path of Marxism-Leninism."

This is strong whispering by the dragon, and the tactics behind it have played into the hands of the men in the Kremlin. For months the Soviet leaders have been telling their own people that the Chinese want a return to Stalinism. Above all else, the peoples of the Soviet Union want nothing that faintly suggests Stalinism.

The Soviet-Chinese argument reached one of its most absurd moments late last year when the Russians turned back a group of Chinese propagandists on the frontier that divides the two countries. The Soviets said the Chinese had boarded a Moscow-bound Russian train loaded with anti-Soviet leaflets.

Peking reacted with a note that said among other things: "The Soviet officials used filthy and vulgar language against girl students and intimidated, insulted and reviled them."

The Russians, on the other hand, accused the Chinese in this same incident of "violating the most elementary rules of sanitation and public hygiene." In less contrived language this means that the once brotherly Chinese urinated on Soviet property, which (as every Soviet citizen is told a thousand times over) means the property of the people.

Most serious of all, perhaps, was the Peking accusation

that Moscow had torn up an atomic bomb agreement to curry favor with the United States. The contract, signed in 1957, was that the U.S.S.R. would give China a sample bomb as well as technical advice and information on its manufacture.

It was broken, thundered the Chinese, in June, 1959. This was three months before Khrushchev went to the United States for the first time and had friendly talks with President Eisenhower. The Chinese statement described Khrushchev's policy as "not peaceful co-existence but capitulationist co-existence."

In any Western evaluation of the break between Moscow and Peking, it should be remembered, as Sir William Hayter, a former British Ambassador to the Soviet Union, has said: "The things that separate Russia from China are still infinitely less than the things which separate us from either of them." He reminded us that Mr. Khrushchev said as late as June, 1963:

"Hatred of class enemies is necessary, because it is not possible to become a good fighter for your people, or for Communism, if one does not know how to hate enemies . . . Yes, Comrades, a harsh class-struggle is now in progress throughout the world. Enemies are attacking our Marxist-Leninist ideology and are attempting to corrupt the spirit and consciousness of the people. And if in this struggle ideological underhand fighters grab us by the elbows or legs, let them not feel offended if these underhand fighters receive blows as well as our open enemies."

No, the Cold War between the West and the Soviet Union is not over. If it is ever to come to an end, the first signs will be the day the Russians take up golf and commence selling Coca Cola in Moscow.

17. When the Pasha Brought Golf to Russia

For years the chances of golf being played in the U.S.S.R. were as remote as the establishment of a stock exchange in Red Square. The Party line on golf was laid down by the formidable Vyacheslav M. Molotov before he fell from grace as Foreign Minister. I remember the occasion well.

Admiral William H. Standley, who was born in Russian River, California, arrived in Kuibyshev in the chilly spring of 1942 to take up his duties as the United States' fourth Ambassador to the Soviet Union. The Admiral flew to Kuibyshev rather than to Moscow because as the German Army closed in on the capital the Russians, for safety reasons, evacuated the diplomatic corps to that flea-bitten city on the Volga.

The Admiral's plane, an old DC3, landed in a snowstorm. One of the most incongruous sights I ever saw in Russia was His Excellency walking from his plane through the snow in Kuibyshev carrying a bag of golf clubs. Shortly after establishing himself in a schoolhouse converted into an Embassy, the new envoy raised the question of golf. He was told that there was no course in Kuibyshev and, when he pressed the point, his aides informed him that as far as they knew there was none in the whole land.

"Then unpack my portable driving cage and put it up," said the Ambassador, "because I want to swing." All that spring he swung—in a driving net erected to the bewilderment of the citizens of Kuibyshev in the Ambassadorial backyard.

When the diplomatic corps was shifted back to Moscow, the golf-hungry Admiral took up the issue of golf with Molotov. Glaring at the envoy through his nose glasses, Mr. Molotov thundered, "Golf is not a game for the people. It is for the idle rich and it will never be played in the Soviet Union." So Admiral Standley never once had the opportunity of getting off a good drive, and it grieved him deeply.

Then, after the war, a new Egyptian Ambassador known as the Red Pasha arrived from Cairo to head his country's diplomatic mission, and he too brought his golf clubs. When he inquired of his staff the directions to the closest golf course, his counsellor gave him a translation of Mr. Molotov's observations on the game—in Arabic.

In his study one summer afternoon the Red Pasha said to me, "Gilmore, I don't care what they say, I'm going to play golf."

"Splendid," I said. "You will be making history, but where are you going to make it?"

"Come," he replied, "follow me."

He called out a few sharp commands and his bag of clubs were brought to his office.

"Get the car ready."

One of his Secretaries summoned the Ambassador's chauffeur.

"Where to, *gospodin* Ambassador?"

"To the country. Go out by the Leningradsky Chausée."

The chauffeur obeyed. After we had driven about twelve or thirteen miles, the envoy spotted a spacious cow field and ordered his driver to halt. The three of us got out of the car and crawled through a barbed wire fence. The Red Pasha took out a driver, set a ball on a tee, took a few practice swings and knocked the hell out of the ball. He got about two hundred and twenty yards, I would say, in the direction of some collective farm.

"Come," ordered the envoy. We followed him and had no trouble in locating the ball.

"See that distant telegraph pole," he said as he selected a No. 2 wood and let fly.

The Red Pasha was a good golfer and made his shots as he called them. After a few minutes of driving and chipping around the pasture, he collected several spectators from the farm. They looked at the Ambassador as if they thought he was crazy, but they followed him from shot to shot.

"What's he doing?" inquired one old peasant.

"He's playing a game," answered the envoy's driver who had commenced to get the knack of being a caddy.

The Red Pasha understood no Russian, so he ignored the questions and played on.

"Who gave him permission to play in our pasture?" one peasant asked.

"Comrade Stalin."

"Comrade Stalin?"

"Yes."

"You mean he selected our collective farm for this foreign gentleman to play his game?"

"Yes, this very farm. You should be honored."

"Why should we be honored?"

"Because," I interrupted, "he has selected your farm, of all places in the Soviet Union, to introduce this great game to your country."

"If he kills a cow, he will be sorry."

"He will kill no cow. That isn't the object of the game."

"What *is* the object of the game?"

"Shhhhhh," hissed the Red Pasha.

We must have walked several miles and the Egyptian must have hit a hundred or more shots, yet he never lost a ball, nor struck a cow, nor hit a collective farmer. When he had finished, he asked which of the spectators were officials of the collective. Two men stepped forward.

"I wish to present a gift to your farm, and thank you for allowing me to play a game that I love," he said.

As these remarks were interpreted, the Red Pasha handed over two hundred roubles. The peasants were overjoyed.

"Come back again, *gospodin*," said one.

"Yes, come back," chimed in the other. "You can even hit a cow if you want to, but you must promise not to injure her."

During the remainder of the long summer the Ambassador often visited the collective farm with his golf clubs and balls. It was a happy arrangement for all concerned. And the Red Pasha never hit a cow.

So far as I know, he is the only man ever to play golf in the Soviet Union. That was a long time ago, however. Then towards the end of the summer of 1963, several Western diplomats breathlessly reported signs of what could be a revolutionary change in the Soviet attitude towards golf.

They said that Russian officials had been sounding them out on the game. "How do you build a golf course?" was the most repeated of their questions.

Earlier in the summer, Yugoslavia, that break-away Communist state, showed the first official interest in the game. The credit for this is due to a young man named Robert Cleveland, Economic Counsellor at the American Embassy in Belgrade. An ardent duffer, Cleveland spread the idea that golf could help President Tito's country in its eager drive to attract more tourists.

Officials of the Yugoslav Government thought it over and decided golf might not be a bad idea—but there were strong hints that, if allowed, it might be for foreigners only. In any case, the Yugoslavs sent to Britain for a civil engineer named John Harris who designs golf courses. Elder citizens of the country recalled that golf was once played in Yugoslavia and some remembered that Prince Paul was a low-scoring player.

"But don't expect a golf boom in this country," warned a Yugoslav journalist who knows his country well. "If Yugoslavs begin to play golf, the high government officials and generals will have to first take up the game. Then perhaps others will follow. But golf will never become a big popular Sunday recreation here. It will never replace soccer."

That is what they once said in the United States, "Golf will never replace baseball." Yet what happened? More Americans now play golf than watch and play baseball or football.

The Hon. James A. Farley, board chairman of the Coca Cola Export Corporation, assures me that he has never received so much as a feeler from the Kremlin on how to build a bottling plant, but it seems that the possibility of the Soviet Union recognizing golf is not so remote. And who knows but what the Russians will take it up as a sport? If they do, I predict they will make excellent golfers. When the cry of "Fore!" rings out across the Great Muscovy Plain, it will only be a question of time before the boys down at the corner will be asking for a kokakolavich.

18. The
Amerikansky Club

In an old red brick building in the heart of Moscow, a group of enthusiastic American extroverts do a superb job of making friends for the United States. On a purely voluntary basis, and in their spare time, they make a home away from home for fellow Americans and scores of foreign diplomats and foreign embassy personnel. Without the warm hospitality of The Amerikansky Club, life in Moscow would be dull and downright lonely for a lot of foreigners, many of them from the uncommitted countries. After a few visits to the gay, informal and friendly club, they go away feeling well disposed to the U.S.A.

The Americansky Club is the Moscow home of American servicemen and clerks attached to the United States Embassy. They live and sleep at the Club. On the second floor the boys have made and decorated a gathering place which is as American as baseball, a high school hop, or *Way Down Upon the Sewanee River*.

It was founded shortly after World War II and it flourished under the encouragement of the late General Walter

Bedell (Beetle) Smith, and Lieut. Gen. John (Iron Mike) O'Daniel, who were respectively United States Ambassador and Military Attaché in Moscow.

The big room is the Club. It shows American movies, holds bingo games, and from its semi-circular bar dispenses what must be the largest drinks in the world. Music is furnished by a juke box whamming out the latest in American jazz. In the past the club had a live orchestra, as I have pointed out, known as The Kremlin Krows.

Two members of the original orchestra are back in the Soviet capital, doing a second stretch, so to speak: Minister-Counsellor John M. McSweeney, a good knockabout bass player, and Military Attaché Col. Peter Leon Urban, a hot fiddler of the Joe Venuti school. The original instruments—furnished by General Lucius Clay when he was the American commander in Berlin—are getting rusty in the basement of the Amerikansky Club. I know, for I carried out an inspection. The trombone is badly sprung. The back of the bass fiddle is broken, and all that is left of the snare drum and the bass drum are a stack of broken rims.

"Get me the piano player," insisted the Ambassador, "and I'll get the instruments."

With the juke box substituting for The Kremlin Krows, the Amerikansky Club jumps fastest on Saturday night.

After the movies the boys stage a dance; between dances they serve hot dogs in the American manner, something very hard to come upon east of the Danube.

Look out across the dance floor and you see a scene that resembles the United Nations in color, creed and politics. Mixed together are Italians, Frenchmen, Africans, Scandinavians, Germans (including some from East Germany who bravely sneak in on occasion), Indians, Pakistanis, Iranians, South Americans, Britons and, of course, Canadians.

There are, however, no Russians. Perhaps the day will come when they too will attend. If this day ever arrives, the Kremlin is going to have some committed comrades in a way it has never suspected.

In mid-February the Soviet Foreign Ministry sent a note to all foreign missions in Moscow announcing that its official guest house, Speridonovka Palace would be open—on a limited basis—for table tennis, chess and the showing of Soviet films.

I looked in at Speridonovka one evening. Compared with the jumping Amerikansky Club, the Russian recreational center was a drab affair.

Some Western diplomats suggested that the Russians made their palace available as a recreational center as a counter attraction to the Amerikansky Club, and its first cousin, the Britansky Club. (The Britansky Club is a less lusty British Embassy version of the Amerikansky.)

I seriously doubt if the Soviets are trying to buck the obvious attractions of the Amerikansky Club, which is located on the north bank of the Moskva River. If the Kremlin really wanted to set up a place to draw diplomats, young and old, away from the American institution, they would lay something on in a very large way, with Russian girls, dancing, vodka and not chess and the lukewarm champagne of Speridonovka Palace served by tired and over-nationalized waiters. In any case, it is not cutting down on the clientele of the club.

Returning to the Amerikansky Club, was, for me, a bit like going home.

I approached the bar and before I could order a drink, one of the two shirt-sleeved American barmen said, "I'm Al, what can I do for you?"

I told him who I was and he said, "Oh, yes, we know about you and Mrs. Gilmore. You had something to do with the founding of our Club, didn't you?"

"Only in the most modest way."

"You've never been modest in your life," laughed Tamara.

"Anyhow, welcome," said Al. "What'll it be, Scotch or bourbon?"

I gave him our order and was staggered at the size of the drinks he poured. "It's on the house," he told us.

"But we can't accept that."

"At least this first time," he said.

Slowly, the big room darkened and the motion picture projector mounted above the bar flashed a title on a screen at the far end of the room.

"My," said a Norwegian girl beside me. "Another prison picture. Don't they have anything in America but prisons and prisoners?"

Al the barman shook his head. "I don't know who picks these pictures for us," he said, "but whoever it is doesn't give much thought to his job. Hell, this whole place over here is a sort of a prison for us, in a way, and we don't need prison movies to remind us of it." Prison films did seem an odd choice for Western audiences in Communist countries.

I looked down. Two full glasses had replaced our empty ones.

"I insist on paying," I said.

"O.K., if you insist."

I handed over the money. Al made a quick calculation at the cash register and handed me back my change. It was precisely the sum I had given him.

"There's a mistake. You've short-changed yourself."

"We never make mistakes."

All through the evening, this same routine was repeated. Every time I ordered a drink, the barman would solemnly accept my money, ring up something on the register, and then hand me back the same amount I had paid him.

"This is getting embarrassing," I said to Tamara.

"Don't be a fool," she told me, "that young man is paying you one of the highest compliments I can think of. Don't spoil it."

The Amerikansky Club is a non-profit-making organization. Its purpose is to entertain and, I suppose, to keep a lot of Americans away from the temptations of Moscow night life. There is not much of it beyond the restaurants and the youth cafés, but in the past there have been some distressing incidents involving Embassy personnel and the Soviets. Over the years, several Americans have been out and out framed. There have been fights with Soviet citizens and a number of ugly incidents involving Americans and the secret police. As a place of entertainment in Moscow, the Amerikansky Club eminently carries out its function. I asked Al about the cost of running the bar.

"We manage to break even. When you sell booze by the drink, it's impossible to lose money. I know. My old man back in Massachusetts is a barkeep."

"You'll lose money if you keep setting up these free drinks for my wife and me."

"Free drinks, Mr. Gilmore?" he said very solemnly. "I don't know what you're talking about. You've paid me for every drink except that first one, which was on the house, and I've taken your money. Won't you have another round?"

"Yes, we will, thank you."

I handed over my money. He rang up something on the register, but this time he handed me back my money—plus the equivalent in roubles of two dollars.

"Good evening, Al," said I, shaking hands across the bar. "I've had a wonderful time and so has my wife, but it's time to go."

He smiled and urged us to return to the Club.

I left the money on the bar and Tamara and I walked down the curved stairway to the ground floor.

"Just a minute," I said. "I want to show you something."

"What?" asked Tamara.

"It's nothing much, but it brings back memories of Tanya."

"Of Tanya?"

"Yep. Come along here."

I led the way down to the basement, opened a door and pointed to the furnace for the Club's central heating.

"Do you remember when Tanya was being followed by the N.K.V.D., and she felt she was about to be arrested?"

"Yes. It was a long time ago, wasn't it?"

"At least fifteen years. Do you remember how she dashed through our kitchen door late one night, terrified that the police were right behind her?"

"You mean the night she brought you that shoebox packed with love letters?"

"That's what I'm talking about. Well, I dumped them in that furnace and saw that everyone of them was burned."

"Why did you do that?"

"If the police had ever gotten their hands on them, they'd have ruined the career of a certain man who's now rather important in the State Department."

"I hope he thanked you."

"I don't think he ever knew what I'd done. In any case, it all worked out well. Tanya was liberated with the rest. I hear she's married and has a child."

"And the young man in the State Department?"

"He too is happily married. Come, it's time to go. We've got a car waiting outside."

When we returned to our hotel, the driver said, "Oh, *gospodin*, here's something a sergeant at the Amerikansky Club asked me to give you."

I took the envelope and opened it in my room.

"Dear Eddy Gilmore," it began. "When you're far away from Moscow buy yourself a cigar with this and remember the Amerikansky Club." Enclosed was the rouble equivalent of the two dollars that I had tried to pay Al, the bartender.

"Well, I'll be damned," I said.

During the grim war years in Moscow, a number of charming Russian girls made life far from grim for a lucky group of American and British young men. Nearly all of the girls were pretty and shapely; some of them were ravishing beauties. A few—but only a few—regularly reported to the secret police, but I seriously doubt if they ever had anything of importance to report. The girls—even those who gave information to the N.K.V.D., and the M.V.D.—jeopardized their freedom by associating with foreigners. At one time or another, all of them were warned by the police and some were given orders with accompanying threats to break off their associations with Westerners. Yet, most of them persisted with their friendships and love affairs with a fatalistic recklessness that is wholly Russian.

Some of these West-East alliances ended in marriage, but many others in terrible tragedy. Sooner or later, ninety-eight per cent of the girls were arrested by Beria's policemen and banished to forced labor camps where they suffered ordeals too terrible to describe. Still other girls were forced to sign the most outrageous accusations against the men they loved.

Back in Moscow, I made it a point to locate as many of these girls as I could, learn the stories of those who had been released, and from them the whereabouts and fortunes of the others. For the most obvious reasons I shall call them by names other than their own.

Maria. The friend of a British Captain who not only abandoned her before she was arrested, but went off with her jewels, promising to sell them in Paris and buy her clothes with the money. Life had been tough on her; her once black hair was streaked with grey and her fresh girlish face was severely lined. She served over three years in a labor camp in Soviet Asia and was twice beaten up and raped by her guards.

Lucia. A small, quiet, dark girl with a pretty turned-up nose and blue eyes. She served her time unspectacularly, as she did nearly everything else. Released in the amnesty after Stalin's death, she married a young painter, and gave tragic birth to a son who was deformed. The boy is an apparently hopeless cripple. She was in love with an American major and he with her.

Irina. The tall, dark, fuzzy-haired screwball of my early Moscow years. In love with a British Major, she served about three years after confessing that she had been spying for the officer. Now completely rehabilitated, she is happily married to a young Russian she described as an abstract poet.

Vera. Beautiful and blonde, with gorgeous cornflower blue eyes and flaxen hair. The girl friend of a Dutch diplomat, she is now married to a middle-aged Russian engineer and they have one child. While her eyes are as blue and lovely as ever, she has taken on at least forty pounds and does not seem to care a hoot. "I'm happy," she laughed, "and my husband thinks I'm beautiful, so why should I worry about my figure?"

Nina. The red-haired, full-figured actress of minor film roles who was in love with an American Air Force officer. She is now as big as a barrel, married and apparently happy. She was one of the first girls to be arrested and her performance, under questioning by the N.K.V.D., was not a very pretty one. "She sang to the police like a nightingale," said one of her friends. "She was responsible for the arrest of many of her friends." The teller of this tale made a face as she added, "You should see her now. She deserves the way she looks—the painted whore."

Tossia. Nina's singing put her right in the middle of the pond, as she expressed it. "After a month or two in a Moscow prison in 1957, I was sent to a camp. Well, I don't want to talk about all the things that happened there, but I got out, and as you see, I am still alive." She is still a beautiful girl with sad dark eyes, living with her widowed mother. "Love affairs?" she replied in answer to my question. "Oh, I manage to keep the kettle boiling, but I've learned my lesson. When I go to bed with a man these days, it's with a Russian."

Lubov. Once desperately in love with a Third Secretary at the British Embassy, she is a physical and mental wreck. She smokes one cigarette after another and has bitten her fingernails so deeply that there are only small, jagged ridges left to gnaw on. "See this scar," she said, pointing to an ugly pinkish line down her left cheek. "I received that during an interrogation at the Lubianka. I refused to confess that I was spying for X. The man who was questioning me threw a steel clipboard at me. I live alone and I work in a newspaper kiosk. Who would want to live with me?"

Galya. She looks little changed, a wonder after all she went through. She was the girl friend of a young American Naval officer. "Our baby was born in prison. Of course, I admitted it was his. But they let the baby stay with me, and life wasn't too bad. I got through it and came back to Moscow and married a young school teacher. He got tuberculosis—and died. No, I never heard a word from (the American) and I'd rather not talk about him." Then her handsome face lit up. "We did have some good times, didn't we? Remember those long summer nights at the *dacha?* Ah, dear youth, you have gone so far away."

Valya. Small, with a beautifully proportioned body and large green eyes, she married an American Army officer in Moscow, but was unable to get an exit visa. When he was transferred to the Pacific, she returned to her mother's two-room apartment, heartbroken and in terror of arrest. She crawled into bed, announced she had become paralyzed from the waist down and, so far as any of her friends knew, did not get out of bed for more than two years. Her husband wrote her many letters to Moscow which went undelivered. Finally in 1952 he was told by the Soviet authorities that she had died. He then married a woman who nursed him when he was wounded in the war, and they had two children. After Stalin's death, when Valya at last convinced herself she would not be arrested, she got up from her bed and began to lead a normal life once more. At this point she wrote to her husband, and when he received her letter he had a breakdown. He is now an alcoholic, living in the Philippines.

Rosa. "As big as a snowman on a collective farm," said her cousin. "She has two gold teeth in the front of her mouth and is very proud of them. She was once adored by a Royal Air Force Squadron Leader who insisted on reading her the poems of W. H. Auden, although she knew hardly a word of English. She is now married to an official of the Soviet railways and has two sons and a daughter."

Natasha. Once blonde and with the figure of a school-boy, her high square shoulders have sagged and her hair has been dyed an ox-blood red. "I served about four years, but you know I've always been good with figures and they made me the camp bookkeeper. It wasn't a bad life. I'll tell you one thing—in prison you certainly learned to know who your friends were, your real friends. I'm afraid a great many of the girls couldn't stand up to the questioning and they, well—they talked." With a sudden expression of pain, she pressed her right side, and said, "I'd rather not talk about those days any more. God of mine, you can't imagine how wonderful it is these days with no one following you and no one listening to your telephone calls. Yes, Eddy Eddyvich, life's a lot better for us all."

19. Panties,
Sputniks
and Policies

I spent two full days shopping in Moscow, for this is the only way to learn about quantity, quality, and prices. You must see for yourself. It is laborious and tiring, but there is no other way.

Since the death of Stalin there has been a remarkable upswing in the Soviet standard of living. By Western standards many things are extremely costly—but this is not the point. The point is that eleven years ago they just could not be bought at any price.

In the early days of the first Russian sputniks, an unusually naive Western diplomat said to a woman member of the ruling Soviet hierarchy: "Yes, Madam, you can make sputniks, but you can't make nylon panties." The woman thought for a moment and replied, "True, Mr. Ambassador, but I think it's going to be a lot easier to go from sputniks to nylon panties than it will be to go from nylon panties to sputniks."

A pioneer in the production of lacy drawers, that particular ambassador's country still has to turn out its first sputnik. Today in Moscow you can purchase all the frilly nylon panties you want at prices ranging from $2.75 to $16.50 for a super pair with a matching slip. High? Of course. But they are not only on sale, they are being bought.

As for refrigerators, ten years ago they were almost as rare as Kentucky bourbon in the Kremlin. Still not easy to get, there are, nevertheless, plenty of them in Soviet apartments.

Here are some current Moscow prices:

One lemon, best grade—35 cents. Second grade—28 cents. Man's shirt—$6.75 to $12.

Man's suit—$77 to $141. A Communist Party official showed me his and said it cost the rouble equivalent of $44, but my long search of Moscow stores failed to reveal any at that price.

Good grade overcoat—$265.

Slacks, narrow and cuffless—$27.50.

Toothpaste—33 cents for a small tube.

Socks—$2.75.

Men's shoes—from $28 to $46. Even at these prices I stood for thirty minutes in Moscow's biggest department store and watched them being bought for cash.

The waiter on my hotel floor disappeared for two hours one morning. When I asked him where he had been, he said, "I heard some new shoes made in Czechoslovakia were on sale at a store not far from here, so I went and got in line."

"Did you get a pair?"

"No, I failed."

"Did they cost too much?"

"They cost 46 roubles."

"What's your salary?"

"My basic salary is 48 roubles a month." (This is about $53.)

"Yet you say you could have paid that price. You astound me."

"I didn't get the shoes because when I got to the counter they had only very big sizes left. It's always that way."

"But I can't understand how if your salary is 48 roubles a month and the shoes cost 46 roubles, you are able to afford them."

"I said my *basic* salary was 48 roubles a month. I get good tips, my wife works, and I pay a very low rent."

Low rent is one of the secrets behind Soviet family budgets. With ninety-nine per cent of the apartments nationalized, a two-room apartment will often rent for as little as seven dollars a month. Still it is a staggering fact of life when one has to pay for a pair of shoes almost the whole sum of one's monthly salary.

Food is also high in Russia. Butter is $1.80 a pound, and cheese is $1.15 a pound. Eggs were not always easy to find. When I visited Moscow's biggest food store, two days in the same week, there were none available. They cost $1.71 a dozen for the best grade, $1.45 for the second, and $1.19 for the third. Bread is 15 cents for a good-sized tasty loaf. Potatoes are 19 cents a pound.

Yet I saw long lines of buyers waving cash before every counter. I watched one man buy thirty lemons at the equivalent of 35 cents each. When I asked why he was buying so many, he gave me the answer my impertinence deserved, "It's none of your business."

Many of these consumer items were not available at any price in Stalin's day. Those that could be bought ten and eleven years ago were from five to ten times as costly as they are now.

Since Stalin's time the work day has been reduced from twelve to ten hours and then to seven, although it is not everyone who has a seven-hour day. There are exceptions. Direct taxation has all but disappeared. Income tax was to have been abolished in 1963, but the authorities had second thoughts.

Flowers remain very expensive. Peonies, for instance, sell

for the equivalent of 56 cents each. I paid nearly seventy cents for one rose, but it was a beauty.

An affluent society is slowly emerging in the Soviet Union, particularly in Moscow and Leningrad. I was entertained in three Russian homes where servants were employed on a six-day basis.

There are even such individuals as baby sitters. A few young women started an agency of their own in Moscow in 1963. This example of private enterprise was crushed after a mere eight weeks, not because it was a private enterprise, but because it was inefficient. The *Economic Journal* denounced the amateur baby sitters in an article five columns long. The authors, two women, said baby sitting should be organized on a national not local scale. They told a tale of little Kostik Volkov, age three. His mother, an engineer, hired a baby sitter who, according to the *Economic Journal*, was not fully qualified. What happened? The baby sitter was a flop—she did not know any bedtime stories! So Kostik cried and bawled until his mother returned home. In no time at all the news got around Moscow—don't hire baby sitters from that agency. Their employes do not know bedtime stories.

In my two days of shopping I found just about every sort of garment that you would find in Europe, but I am not certain just how genuine they were as consumer items.

Late in 1963 an investigation revealed that in twenty-six Soviet cities show windows and show cases with luxury items were, alas, samples only. The investigating officials said fashionable clothes and shoes on show at these places were a gigantic confidence trick. In the twenty-six cities the investigators learned that the glittering models were either not produced at all, or made in miserly quantities, or in wholly unserviceable qualities.

Beautifully embroidered children's rompers and well-cut suits were so exclusive they could not be bought. Kid leather shoes for women were not being mass-produced. Those on sale were made especially for the style shows.

Soviet factory managers and workers receive cash bonuses if they exceed planned production targets. New lines mean trouble and cannot be turned out in bonus-gathering quantities. Said Chief Engineer V. V. Goravneva of a Leningrad fur factory, when interviewed by the magazine *Krokodil:* "Do you think we want to lose the money incentives for the sake of those model coats and hats?" That is candor, but it is not goods.

In June 1963 the Soviet government announced that it was undertaking a major reform of industry. High priority, the government insisted, would be given to what it called the more progressive branches of industry, with particular stress on the chemical industry and the production of civilian goods.

The government said the state planners had been told to draw up new plans for 1964 and 1965—and subsequent years. The factories were to turn out more plastics, artificial fibres, glass fibres, synthetic rubber, and synthetic spirits.

As announced, the plan would be to expand greatly the production of clothing, footwear and other consumer goods.

Having heard all this a great many times before, the average Soviet citizen was not greatly impressed. He will wait and see.

Numerous dilemmas face Mr. Khrushchev. Many outstanding young men and women say that the solid material advances are not enough. They want more freedom of expression. Aware of this, the men in the Kremlin fear that if the millions get it, and get their automobiles, and television sets too, and generally live a lot easier than they do now, that old enemy—bourgeois mentality—will arise. It is a whopping big problem—how to give the people personal rewards, while keeping them Communists.

Stationed in Moscow from 1951 to 1955 was one of the West's most brilliant diplomats. He was a great student of the U.S.S.R., the Communist Party and the Soviet people and he read and spoke Russian extremely well.

During his first two years in the tricky Moscow post, where he had served years before in a minor capacity, he made so many correct predictions about Russian affairs that he became known and respected among Kremlinologists all over the world. His prognostications came true with such regularity that he, as well as many others, began to believe that his judgment was infallible. He became almost recklessly confident. When the other diplomats and foreign correspondents had few or no Soviet contacts and sources, he maintained several as well as a few in Eastern European Embassies.

When Stalin was stricken, the majority of his ambassadorial and ministerial colleagues made all sorts of guesses and speculation as to who would be the successor to the old dictator, but Ambassador Z, the Soviet expert, differed from them all, insisting that it would be two of Stalin's associates, not one, who would inherit the task of ruling the Soviet Union and the Party.

We all searched for straws in the Moscovy wind and when, at Stalin's funeral, Malenkov, Beria and Molotov elbowed the others out of the way and made the orations about the dead leader from atop the Lenin tomb, Ambassador Z appeared to have pulled it off again. Many experts guessed Malenkov, but only Ambassador Z said two men would take over.

"Malenkov and Beria have made a deal," His Excellency assured me, "and you can write this with certainty."

"I could write it," I told him, "but it wouldn't get through the censor. Neither will any other speculation on this subject."

"Well," said the envoy, "I've sent my prediction to my Foreign Minister and I believe that time will prove that I am right."

Shortly after this, Ambassador Z went to London for a conference of Ambassadors from his country, and dominated the conference as he expounded his answer to a question that was being asked everywhere.

Ambassador Z's colleague in London disagreed with the

Malenkov-Beria theory and said so, much to the annoyance of the man who had been correct so many times. My friend from Moscow was so upset that the Ambassador in London saw things differently, that he called aside one of the members of the London staff and told him that he truly felt sorry for anyone who had to work under a chief of mission as stupid—and that is the word he used—as the head of the London Embassy.

As life would have it, it was at just this moment that Moscow Radio announced that Beria had been arrested as a traitor and an agent for a foreign power. Ambassador Z, I am assured, heard the startling news in stunned silence, and then raising his hands to his head, cried out, "My God, I'm ruined."

His friends sought to console him. He brushed them aside.

"No, no," he moaned in a voice of utter dejection, "I must resign. That's the only way out."

"Nonsense," said his London colleague, the one who had been rashly described as stupid. "We all make mistakes about Russia."

"Not like this one."

"Oh, yes."

Persuaded not to hand in his resignation, which he seriously considered doing, Ambassador Z returned to his Moscow post and, I am told, never wrote an interesting dispatch on the Soviet Union again.

It is not only with predictions that you can go wrong about Russia.

During the coldest climate of the Cold War, when the Soviet government would hardly give a diplomat instructions on how to find the Foreign Ministry, an intelligent and eager man arrived to take over his country's small mission as Chargé d'Affaires.

Several weeks after his arrival I met him at a Moscow diplomatic party. "Did you know," he asked in a conspiratorial whisper, "that Moscow is being swept by some terrible epidemic?"

"No," said I. "What is it?"

"I'm not sure, but people are dying like flies."

"Are you sure?"

"I'm positive."

"How can you be sure? And do forgive me for asking you this."

He moved very close to me and said, "I see the coffins. Every day. Every day they pass my house by the dozens. People carrying away their dead."

At this point my wife asked, "I'm sorry, but what embassy are you from?"

He told her.

"Oh, dear me," said Tamara, letting him down as lightly as she could. "You live only a few doors from the central coffin dispensary of Moscow."

"What?" he gasped.

"Yes. These are hard days. When you need a coffin for someone you have to go and get it. They don't deliver them."

The diplomat groaned. "That must be it. You know how it is with a small embassy. We don't have much to do, so I stand there at my big picture window that looks out on the busy street—and I watch all Moscow go by, and so much of it goes by with a coffin."

"Well, no harm done," I said.

He looked very gloomy. "I'm not so sure. You see I've sent a dispatch about the epidemic to my Foreign Minister."

"If you'll take a bit of advice from a correspondent," I ventured, "do nothing about it."

"No?"

"No. I doubt if the Russians will deny it, because, unless they're breaking your code, they won't know anything about your dispatch. I mean they won't deny it."

"I see."

About a week had gone by when I next saw him. He drew me into a corner and asked, "You remember the epidemic?"

"Yes."

"Well, I have received a message from my Foreign Ministry about it. They congratulated me. I wanted to thank you for suggesting that I shouldn't explain to them what really happened. But tell me, do you still think the Russians will do nothing about it?"

"Of course they won't do anything about it, for they won't know anything about it."

They never did.

The man who discovered the epidemic in Moscow is now an Ambassador in one of the world's great capitals. He is still regarded as something of a Russian expert, and in his dossier at his Ministry of Foreign Affairs there is, I feel quite certain, a commendatory notation, dated 1949, for singular enterprise in the U.S.S.R.

I cite these two stories not to ridicule two diplomats, men I know to be intelligent and hard-working civil servants of their respective countries. I have told them to point out the difficulty of interpreting correctly things that one sees and hears in the Soviet Union.

If you want to speculate on what is going to happen in Moscow, then predict what is going to happen tomorrow, or the day after tomorrow, but not next week, next month, or especially next year. You are fairly safe if you predict what is going to take place in, say, twenty years time because if you are completely wrong, no one is likely to remember or care after twenty years.

Having lost both Stalin and the Revolution, the Soviet state is undergoing deep social changes and I predict it will undergo many more. The Russians did not lose the Revolution because of their historical break with the Chinese Communists. I think the Soviets lost the Revolution when they let Joseph Broz Tito defy them in Yugoslavia and show the Communist world that there are more ways of running a so-called Communist country than by blindly and obediently executing every order from Moscow.

The Kremlin also made a major and irrevocable blunder in asking Peking for advice—and heeding it—during the challenges of the Polish and Hungarian uprisings. This let the Chinese into Europe. Having got into Europe, what was more natural for the Chinese than to dream of going into Africa, Southeast Asia, and even into Cuba and South America?

The issues dividing Moscow and Peking are extremely complex, when looked upon as the clashing of two ideologies competing over interpretations of Karl Marx and Lenin. They are not very complicated if the Russians and the Chinese are regarded as old-fashioned imperialists, driven by the age-old ambitions and objectives that have always motivated imperialist empires in the past.

With the loss of Yugoslavia—because of Tito—and the loss of Albania—principally because of Mao Tse-tung—Imperialist Communist Russia has learned a great truth. It is this: inasmuch as conquest of the world is no longer possible, is it not vastly more preferable to have absolute neutrals than wobbly and costly satellites?

Is not Finland, for instance, a far better investment than Hungary, Poland or Romania, into which the Soviet Union has poured millions and must pour more millions if their present relationship to Moscow is to be continued?

Then there is this perplexing possibility of a real and lasting peace. Because both the Russians and the West fully comprehend the horrible consequences of a nuclear war, such a war is out of the question. The chances of peace are better today than they have been for years. It is my opinion that we shall see local wars, perhaps, but never again a world war.

The very fact that there is no alternative to peace has given new dimensions to statesmanship, and is revolutionizing thinking in the chancelleries of the world. For the first time in seven thousand years, the leaders of nations realize, or are coming to realize, that they must now think in terms of peace and not in terms of war. War, the ultimate weapon of the past, can never again be relied upon, or even contemplated, as a "solution" to the differences between powers.

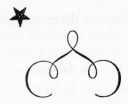

20. Joseph Stalin
and Nikita Khrushchev

On March 5th, 1963—the tenth anniversary of Joseph Stalin's death—the Soviet Union ignored the passing of a decade with contemptuous indifference.

Round anniversaries, such as the tenth, twentieth, and thirtieth of the births and deaths of prominent persons are always noted in the U.S.S.R., and one would have thought that the milestone would have been mentioned in the press to say the least. Yet the Communist Party newspaper *Pravda*, of which Stalin was a founding editor, gave him not so much as a cold line of copy, and neither did any other newspaper. Moscow Radio, which once heralded Stalin's activities to the far corners of the world, was mute.

Stalin was a merciless tyrant and worse, but he was the originator of the Soviet Union's planned national economy, the architect of the Red Army's victory in World War II, and the man who did more than any other to industrialize a backward agricultural country, but the tenth anniversary of his death went as unnoticed as, well, the birthday of the late Senator Joseph McCarthy.

How vividly I remembered his funeral, the mass mourning in Red Square, Stalin's closest associates marching into Red Square with their dead leader's body encased in a coffin with a transparent bubble top, Chou En-lai's impassive face at the head of the column of marchers, beside Georgi Malenkov and L. P. Beria, and how the body was laid to rest in the great red tomb in Red Square beside the embalmed body of V. I. Lenin.

I asked a Russian friend, a college professor, why there was complete silence on the anniversary.

"It surprises me too," he replied. "I would have thought that certain people would still be so happy over his passing away that something might have been done about it."

"No," said his wife. "Stalin is something we've all got to forget for a long number of years. One day, yes, his correct place in the history of this country will be found, but not now. If Russia is to live with the rest of the world, if we are to live with ourselves, we've got to forget him."

"Perhaps," said her husband.

I remembered that this couple's only son had been executed in one of Stalin's purges.

"I'm sorry," I said, "but we'll drop the subject if you prefer."

"Oh, no, don't. It's all part of Russia, all a part of being Russian."

"Oddly," said the professor who is now an old man, "public mention was made today of the tenth anniversary of Prokofiev's death."

"Vanya," asked the wife, "did Prokofiev die on the same night as Stalin?"

"Indeed, he did," said I, "and I suspect that he died of a broken heart, and that Stalin, more than anyone else broke it."

"Yes," said the wife, "he hated Prokofiev. Do you suppose it was because the composer was a Jew?"

"That had something to do with it," said her husband, "but it was more than that. It was Prokofiev's music. Stalin's

tastes in music were simple. He didn't understand Prokofiev's music—so he hated him."

"Would you say that Mr. Khrushchev hates modern art
because he doesn't understand it?" I asked.

"I don't think Khrushchev hates modern art," said the
professor. "He doesn't understand it—and I might say
neither do I—but I don't think either of us hates it, or the
people who practice it."

"I never knew Prokofiev died on the same night as did
Stalin," the wife repeated.

"Well, I do," I told her, "for it was in trying to write
about Prokofiev's death that I received my cruelest piece of
censoring from the Soviet censor."

"Yes?"

"Well, I tried to couple the two deaths in a dispatch to
my office in America. 'Only in Russia,' I wrote, 'could Peter
and the Wolf die on the same night.' "

"And only in Russia they would," smiled the professor.

Stalin's body was, of course, removed from beside Lenin's
on the night of October 31st, 1961, and buried in the small
cemetery between the tomb and the Kremlin's east wall.
The body lies beneath a slab of black stone on which is
written:

J. V. STALIN

1879–1953

March 5th, 1963 was a cold day. About two inches of
snow fell early in the morning. At ten o'clock that morning
there was still snow on Stalin's grave. By noon it had been
swept clean. Then something strange happened.

Western newspapermen made a point of visiting Stalin's
grave every hour or so. At least one journalist, an American,
went to the Novodevichy Monastery near the Moskva
River, about four miles from the Kremlin, to visit the grave
and marble monument of Nadezhda, one of Stalin's wives.

(Nadezhda had died in 1932 at the age of 31 by suicide or murder.) He found lying on her grave a small bouquet of mimosa.

A Russian friend, who should know, told me the mimosa was placed there by Stalin's daughter, Svetlana. Later in the day, a British correspondent reported that a similar spray of mimosa had been put on Stalin's grave. My friend told me that Svetlana, who loved her father and was loved by him, was also responsible for this gesture.

Then an hour or so later, another Western correspondent —not an American—said that he saw a small wreath on Stalin's grave. In connection with this, an unusual rumor was whispered around the foreign colony. One correspondent, who on March 4th had scored a beat on the Moscow representative of a rival newspaper, put it about that his competitor, seeking to get his revenge, placed the wreath there himself—and then wrote about it. His story was exclusive for several hours.

In any case, neither the spray of mimosa, nor the wreath, remained on Stalin's grave very long. By early sundown the grave was as coldly bare as it was at sunrise.

God knows I have no reason or wish to say a word in defense of Joseph Stalin, but what happened in Red Square —and what did not happen—ten years after his demise adds a shabby little footnote to the story of one of history's most amazing men.

"I can tell you one thing for sure," said an American newspaperman whose opinions on Russia I respect, "if you want to get kicked out of this country write something about the old man that he doesn't like."

"By the old man, you mean Crush?" I asked.

"Who's Crush?"

"Spell it with a K," I said, "then it comes easier. When Mr. Khrushchev and Mr. Bulganin visited Britain, some man of brilliance referred to them as Crush and Bulge."

"I agree," said my colleague, "but don't call him Crush or Khrush over here. I don't think he would like it, and if he doesn't like it, out you go."

"But no one would be booted out for something as innocuous as that."

"Perhaps not, but you'd be getting close."

"Oh God, then he's getting like Stalin about personal references?"

"It's not that bad."

"When Khrushchev was on a visit to Vienna I saw him doze at the opera and I reported it—"

"Then I'm a little surprised they let you back in."

I reminded him I was in Moscow as a tourist.

"That probably explains your presence," said my friend.

I related to him how, after the dozing incident, a member of Mr. Khrushchev's party in Vienna approached me, and it was during a ceremony in the town hall, and with a deep frown said, "He's a very, very good person. You should not write bad things about him."

"What bad things have I written?"

"You wrote that he dozed at the opera last evening."

"What's that got to do with his being a good or bad person?"

"I repeat," said the Soviet official, "he's a very good person, and he's doing a great deal for our country."

"I agree," I said, "but if President Kennedy should doze at a baseball game at Yankee Stadium—and I saw it—I would report it. If Queen Elizabeth sneaked a short nap at the Royal Opera House—and I saw it—I'd report it."

"Such reporting is not the job of a correspondent," said the official, his frown practically cutting his forehead in two. "That's the sort of personal journalism that isn't journalism."

"I'm sorry, we differ."

Flashing me a quick frigid smile, the official walked quickly away.

After relating this incident, I said to my colleague in

Moscow, "Then I don't suppose you write very much about Mr. Khrushchev's successor?"

"Not from Moscow."

"Who *is* going to succeed him?"

"If a successor had to be named today, it would be Kozlov."

"Oh, I disagree," said an official from the British Embassy. "Kozlov's a sick man."

"I still say Kozlov."

"And what about you?" I asked an American diplomat.

"I'll take a dark horse. I'll say Suslov."

Someone laughed.

"What about you?" asked my newspaper friend.

"How the hell would I know?"

"If it comes to that," smiled the American, "how the hell would any of us know?"

"That's candor, friend," said I.

"All right," said the Englishman, "what's your guess?"

"Shepelin or Polyansky," I said. "It's going to be a young man."

A Belgian diplomat spoke up. "You didn't ask me, but I say it's going to be Brezhnev."

Speculating on Khrushchev's successor is more difficult than guessing Stalin's successor.

"In any case," said my newspaper colleague, "it is not going to be terribly important who succeeds him immediately. The important thing will be the man who takes over the job after the first year or two. Remember what happened after Stalin—Malenkov, Bulganin and then Khrushchev, and Khrushchev had some tight squeezes, but he's in now, in like Flynn."

Difficult or easy, speculating on Khrushchev's successor is, in a way, a waste of time. The outside world has such little real information about the personal relationships of the high members of the Communist Party, little or no information on cliques within the Central Committee, and very few facts about the health of the individuals who make up the hierarchy of the Party.

At best, it's a guessing game.

Here are a few sample headlines on the subject, printed fairly recently above stories by thoroughly competent newspapermen: NEO-STALINISTS PLOTTING TO OUST KHRUSHCHEV; CHINA GROUP IN KREMLIN OUT FOR K'S SCALP; SOVIET PREMIER STILL REBUKED FOR CUBA CLIMB-DOWN; RUSSIAN LEADER RAPPED FOR LETTING CHINESE SITUATION GET OUT OF HAND; K'S DAYS NUMBERED, PLOTTERS SAY; KHRUSHCHEV, 70, SOON TO STEP DOWN.

I could quote a dozen more. I could also cite other ways of spelling his last name. Some say Khrushchev, others say Kruchev. Krushchov is the way it sounds in Russian, and that is the way I have seen it in many Soviet publications printed in the English language.

I asked countless questions of Russians about the state of affairs within the powerful Central Committee of the Communist Party of the Soviet Union, and not from one person did I receive the slightest suggestion of a rustle of rebellion against the man now leading the country. Everything I saw and heard in the U.S.S.R. convinced me that Mr. Khrushchev is firmly entrenched as the Soviet leader. He is 70 and we may draw the obvious conclusions from that. He drives himself fairly hard and he cannot go on for a great many years.

The Soviet leader is an amazing man. He is an extremely adroit politician. Barring the late John F. Kennedy, I never saw a better one, or one who works at politics with more consistency. Mr. Khrushchev is an extremely good public speaker—when he does not lose his temper. When that happens, and it is happening with less frequency now, he splutters and overstates his case.

In bad temper or good, he has a facile way of bringing all sorts of issues down to earth with a bang, usually with some simple country aphorism. He is a supreme master of quotation. Lesser speakers drag quotations into their speeches by the heels, with awkward pauses and tricky transitions, but not Khrushchev. Scolding his agricultural bureaucrats recently he thundered, "Don't send your directives to collective farm cows—they cannot read."

In recent years he has cut down on his drinking. I know a man who takes notes on his imbibing. "He's down to sipping white wine," he told me. "Gone are the old days of dozens of toasts in vodka."

From what I could tell, a collective of a sort does exist in the Kremlin, with Khrushchev of course at the top. Yet in an emergency, Khrushchev can and does call the shots.

In connection with Khrushchev's decisions, I found agreement among several foreign diplomats—men who have been around the Soviet Premier for a year or more—that Mrs. Nina Khrushchev, the cultured, motherly and charming wife of the Premier, has weighty influence with her husband.

"I have positive evidence," Ambassador X told me, "that her opinion on several occasions has changed the mind of her husband over night. Mind you, I'm not saying this applies to big policy decisions."

I call him Ambassador X because even the suggestion that Mrs. Khrushchev can influence the Prime Minister might be interpreted in Moscow as being disparaging to him. In an ancient patriarchy such as Russia, to imply that a woman may have the power to sway the thought processes of her husband, could be interpreted as impolite, or even outrageous.

He is a man of great contradictions. Sometimes he will explode in a bluster of denunciation, and charge his language with spicy and even vulgar expressions. Again, when something happens that might be expected to provoke him, he will give the gentlest of answers.

I cite his broadside at Soviet abstract artists the day he visited the big show of Soviet modern art. Khrushchev to the young painter Zheltovsky:

"You're a nice looking fellow, but how could you paint

something like this? We should take down your pants and put you in a clump of stinging nettles until you understand your mistakes. You should be ashamed. Are you a pederast or a normal man? Do you want to go to a foreign country? All right, go on then. We'll take you free as far as the frontier. Go on, live out there in what they call 'the free world.' Yes, live in and study in the school of capitalism, and then you'll know what's what. But I'll tell you, we aren't going to spend a kopeck on this dog shit. We have the right to send you out to cut trees until you've paid back the money the State has spent on you!"

Yet a young Soviet writer told me that in the controversy over modern art and writing, Khrushchev has on several occasions played a fairly moderating role.

"There have been several cases where authors have been unable to get their books published," he said. "When all else failed, they managed to get through to Comrade Khrushchev. After they approached him and stated their case, they received permission to publish. He gave it in a sort of 'all right, go on and print it, it won't hurt anything' attitude."

I asked if Mrs. Khrushchev might have had anything to do with her husband's decision. "Since you mention it, yes, she might have," was his reply.

I cited recent repressions.

"One thing is certain," he said. "The new creative forces let loose over here—they're going to be hard to stop. I don't think anyone can stop them."

The Soviet leader may have his detractors and even severe critics among the Party, but with the great majority of the Soviet people I talked to he had their admiration, respect, and affection.

21. The Blonde
in Uniform

After twenty-three years of being a foreign correspondent, travelling in many lands on generous expense accounts, and undergoing the hospitable exploitation of several kind millionaires in some of the world's lushest oases, I have formed a number of rock-hard prejudices about a few of the more enjoyable features of life, from which the logic of experts, superiors, friends and acquaintances can never sway me.

I am utterly convinced that Belgians brew the best beer, that Scots distill the purest whisky, that French wines are superior to all others, that the most succulent ham comes from Virginia, and that for fruit and vegetables no one can beat the Italians. London tailors make the best men's clothes, the dressmakers of Geneva the finest gowns, Americans the tastiest of all steaks, and Germans the most efficient automobiles. Finally, when it comes to interpreting and presenting and acting the wonderful plays of Anton Chekhov, there are no people on earth like the members of the Moscow Art Theatre.

Despite the discomfort of its hard, straight-back wooden seats, an evening of Chekhov at the slightly musty green and white building on a Moscow side street is one of life's most agreeable experiences.

One must dine early, for the curtain rises at 6:30 P.M., and if one goes there on an empty stomach, the abdominal rumblings may seriously interfere with the verbal music sweeping from the stage through the lips of the most polished of performers.

For our return to this theatre where Tamara and I spent so many pleasant hours in the past, we chose "The Cherry Orchard." The great Tarasova played Madame Ranevskaya, and as she has been doing the part for many years, I thought she looked surprisingly well preserved. Of course, A. H. Gribov, a real professional if there ever was one, was superb as Firs. Yet as fascinated as one becomes with the artistry of the actors and actresses, the magic of Chekhov dominates the stage from the opening to the final line—and then lingers on.

I always marvel at his sentimentality, so completely without self-pity; the hopelessness of everyone and everything and the futility of life in the Russian countryside, as real under Communism as before the Revolution—but for different reasons. Then the great idea of "The Cherry Orchard" itself, for is not life itself a cherry orchard, with the dreams and fancies of childhood that never materialize, the lost days of youth, the never-recaptured innocence of childhood and the inevitability of decay, always so gentle with this genius among Russian writers?

The audience was awful, however. They laughed at the wrong places and, one felt, generally failed to understand the play. At the first interval I asked an old Russian friend about this.

"Well," he said, "they've been presenting Chekhov so many, many years, always as Stanislavsky wanted him presented, that the intelligentsia has grown tired of seeing him."

"Really," I asked with some astonishment, "can anyone ever tire of Chekhov?"

"Yes, my friend. If you're a Russian and living in Russia."

"I hadn't thought of it that way. Yes, you have a point."

"I'm sure I have. So, with the intelligentsia staying away, what do you get here? The factory workers and the provincials. But they'll learn, and then they'll get bored with it all, for I'm sure the Moscow Art Theatre will never change. I for one hope it won't."

At this point a young American officer and his pretty blonde wife came up to us. My old Russian friend bowed quickly and left. I tried to stop him, but he was gone.

"Good evening," said the young man. "You remember I met you and your wife at a cocktail party shortly after you arrived from London."

"Of course."

As we shook hands, I happened to glance over the husband's shoulder and I thought I saw something that I had not seen since returning to Moscow. It was, I felt certain, a secret policeman and he was watching us.

"Who is he following," I asked myself, "the Captain (he was an Air Force Officer) or me?"

And then I remembered. This young man had been accused in the Soviet press of being involved in collecting secret information from Oleg Penkovsky. I knew this was no small matter even then. Later, as the world knows, Penkovsky was shot for spying against the Soviet Union, and the British businessman, Greville Wynne, allegedly involved in the same business, was sentenced to eight years imprisonment for espionage.

"Won't you have some candy?" asked the Captain, holding out a small box of chocolates.

"Thank you," I replied and as I reached into the box, I saw the secret policeman stiffen and make a big mental note—or so I thought—of what he saw.

As we chatted along, all the while I grew, to my shame, more and more nervous. "The Captain and his wife," I thought to myself, "have diplomatic passports and therefore immunity from arrest. Tamara and I, like businessman Wynne, have ordinary passports and are liable to arrest on any sort of charge that the Soviets feel like presenting."

Fortunately, the bell rang and we all returned to our seats. Captain X and his wife were on one side of the theatre, Tamara and I on the other. Back in my seat in the fourth row, with Tamara beside me, I felt somehow ashamed that I had all but panicked at this casual meeting with a man who had been denounced as being involved in espionage, untrue though this may have been. I was determined to say nothing of my fears to Tamara.

At the next interval I asked Tamara if she would mind if we stayed in our seats.

"Why?"

"It's my stomach," I said. "You know, I didn't eat anything before coming over here."

"It hasn't bothered me."

"No, I don't know why it is, but why growl not the bowels of the young?"

"You're being affected by Chekhov."

"That's not Chekhov."

"It certainly isn't, but I'm sorry if your stomach hurts. That's all right, we'll have a big dinner when we get back to the hotel."

Since we stayed put, I was able to avoid the pleasant young Captain and his wife for the rest of the evening. I hope he did not notice it.

As we left the theatre and strolled towards our hotel, I worked every trick I remembered to detect whether I was being followed. I dropped my glove and turned quickly to pick it up—and looked behind me. I walked around a corner, did an about face and retraced my steps.

"Hoaney," asked Tamara with an anxiousness in her voice I had not heard for a long time, "is it—are we being followed?"

"I just want to make sure."

"Well, are we?"

"No, I don't think so."

"What made you think we were?"

"I didn't think we were. I only wanted to be sure."

"When did you notice someone?"

"Back at the theatre."

"Oh, God."

"Don't worry, darling. There's absolutely nothing to worry about."

"Nothing to worry about? Hoaney, they might not let me out of here."

"Come on, Tomka. There's absolutely nothing to worry about."

I then told her about the Captain. "I think," I explained, "that he was being followed."

Tamara said nothing. We had one more corner to turn before we reached the hotel. As we went around it, I took her arm and we halted. I pretended we were looking at something in a shop window. We waited for several minutes. When no one appeared from around the corner, I sighed a deep sigh of relief.

"There's no one," I said. "Of that I'm sure. Come on, let's go have dinner."

In the warmth of the Restaurant National and in the infectious gaiety of the dancers and the music, we both relaxed.

During the ten years that we had lived away from Moscow, there was one question that Tamara asked with tiresome regularity: "When may I go back home?"

Despite the fact that we had lived in the United States and London for a decade, Moscow was still home to my wife and I hope that it was only natural that this often worried me. I nagged myself with self-questioning. "Where have I failed?" I would ask and then, the old saying,

"Russians make the world's worst immigrants" would go through my mind.

Tamara's home in the West had been a series of homes and perhaps, I said to my wounded conscience, this is the trouble.

When we first got away from Russia, we lived in my birthplace of Selma, Alabama, in a delightful cottage on a beautiful hillside, made available to us through the characteristic kindness of Alice and Charles Hohenberg. Then after a year, when my wife became an American citizen in fact, we moved to London and there for four years we occupied a charming Queen Anne house in Chelsea's Cheyne Row. With the birth of our third daughter, Natasha, Tamara asked me one winter evening if I had ever counted the number of steps from our cellar kitchen to the top of the house.

"Never," I replied. "Should I?"

"There are fifty-six steps from the bottom to the top, and to put it bluntly, my feet are beginning to ache."

"You, a onetime ballerina, suffering from tired feet?"

"The same muscles are not used."

"All right, we'll move."

"And while I'm asking questions, when may I go back home?"

"You mean go back to Moscow?"

"Off korse."

"When it's safe for you to go back. You remember how long it took to get you out this time? We don't want to go through that again, do we?"

"No, but I'd like to see my family again."

"I'm sure you would, darling. Just as soon as I feel sure that there will be no trouble, I'll see what can be done."

"That's what you always say."

"I know, darling, but it does worry me. Would you return without me?"

"Oh, no."

"Then let's wait a little while longer."

From Chelsea we moved to a penthouse atop the highest point in London. There for four years we enjoyed one of the most superb views in the United Kingdom, but the question continued to be raised, "When may I go back home?"

"But, Tamara, this is home."

"Hardly," she would say. "As beautiful as it is, it's not Moscow, and furthermore, it's not a real home of my own."

"You mean we should buy a home in England?"

"I love England. I also love Russia. I suppose Moscow will always be home to me."

"I'm sorry."

"Oh, hoaney, I don't mean it that way. You and the children are everything, but—"

"Yes, I know, you're a Russian at heart."

In the spring of 1962, we bought a part Tudor, part Elizabethan house in Sussex, with the front door opening into the picturesque High Street of East Grinstead and the rear doors and Tudor windows looking out upon uninterrupted views of the Ashdown Forest four miles away.

"Do you still want to go home?" I asked when we had installed ourselves.

"This is wonderful, but—"

"Yes, I know. Moscow's still home."

Then came the opportunity to make this return trip to Moscow. As our visit began to near its scheduled conclusion, I was sitting at the desk in the living-room of our hotel suite, writing my diary of the previous day, when Tamara returned from her daily trip to see her family.

"Hoaney," she said as she laid a hand on my shoulder, "I want to go home."

"Will you please say that again?"

"I said I want to go home."

I am afraid a tear or two formed in my eyes as well as hers.

"I've always wanted to hear that from you."

"Well, I mean it, darling. Seeing Mama and Zina and Vovo and all the rest of them has been wonderful, but I've realized where home is."

I took her in my arms.

"You know," I said, "we should think about packing. Our plane leaves day after tomorrow."

"Hoaney?" Her big brown eyes were clouded with worry.

"No," I tried to assure her, "there won't be any trouble. They'll recognize your American passport. You'll see."

On the last day, after the most tearful of family farewells, we hurried back to the National, locked the last bags, stuffed away an armload of presents that had been pressed upon us at the last moment, and called for the porters. It was Luba the chambermaid, however, who appeared before the porters.

"And now you're going?"

"God and British European Airways willing," I replied.

"And the Soviet Union," said Tamara in English under her breath.

In the old familiar Russian manner, Luba asked us to be seated, just as Tamara's mother had done but a few minutes before. Standing over us, she blessed us with her right hand, crossed herself and whispered a prayer for safety on our journey.

"Thank you, Luba."

"Well," she said, "it's all over. You're on your way." Then she startled me by enveloping me in her bearlike arms, kissing me on both cheeks and exclaiming, "*Golubchik, dosvidania!*"

I over-tipped her. Naturally.

After more farewells—and more tips—down the corridor, in the elevator, at the reception desk, at the front door, we at last loaded ourselves and our luggage into an Intourist automobile and headed for the international airport in a snowstorm.

It was a long and mostly silent drive behind a totally silent driver.

Reaching the reception center, I paid off the chauffeur and thanked him.

"I'll wait," he said, "you might need me."

Feeling the way I did, even this remark seemed sinister.

"Yes," I said, "we might not take off. It's snowing very hard, isn't it?"

"Yes it is, *gospodin*."

I counted six passengers, including Sol Hurok, ahead of us. I also sighted one of those big and bumptious blondes who seem to attach themselves to, or are attached by, the Soviet Union's civil air transport system. On closer look, however, I realized she was either customs, or security, or both.

"How many passengers are we?" I asked.

"How many do you see?" she snapped.

"Six," I answered. "Eight with us."

"I see that you can count," was her comment.

She took our passports, tossed Tamara's aside and began a page-by-page examination of mine. Satisfied that it was in order, she snapped it shut and placed it atop five other passports.

"That," I said, "is my wife's."

"I can read."

With that she handed me two forms to fill out and motioning with her head said, "Over there. Complete them."

Earlier I had told Tamara that in her dealings with the customs and security officials at the airport to speak nothing but English. In her nervousness, I suppose, she forgot. In any case, as I was filling in the forms, I heard the blonde in the uniform say:

"I'll ask the questions, you'll do the answering."

I looked up. Tamara must have said something in Russian for the blonde fairly shouted:

"What's this? You speak Russian without an accent, yet you have an American passport?"

"I'm an American citizen," said Tamara in English.

"You speak Russian, I heard you. Come on, speak Russian."

"I said I was an American citizen." This was in Russian.

"You have an American passport," said the woman, searching through Tamara's document, "but here it says you live in England. Yes, and here—well, where were you born?"

I hurried over to the counter. "Is all this really necessary?" I asked as calmly as I could. "We are American citizens, visiting the Soviet Union as tourists, why all the questions?"

"I ask the questions," she repeated. "When I want either of you to answer then I'll ask you. Now, you were born somewhere. Where?"

"I was born in Moscow."

"You were born in Moscow. You have an American passport and you live in England."

"What the hell's wrong with that?" I demanded.

"I'm not talking to you."

"Well, I'm talking to you."

"Tovarich Smetanov," she shouted to a man in a blue uniform, "Tovarich Smetanov, come over here!"

I noticed that this little scene was being witnessed by a tall young man in the uniform of British European Airways (BEA). Silently praying that he was an Englishman, I walked over to him and asked in English, "Is there anything you can do to halt this little third degree?"

"All rather unpleasant, isn't it?"

"It surely is."

He disappeared, but within a matter of minutes the loud-speakers came alive.

"Will all London passengers please proceed to doorway A?" said a voice in English. "Your plane will leave in five minutes. Please hurry along."

He repeated the announcement in Russian.

As I walked back to the counter where the blonde,

Tamara and Tovarich Smetanov were huddled, I saw the blonde toss her head as she gave me a defiant look.

"That's all," said Smetanov, "and you'd better hurry. You may hold up the plane."

I took Tamara's arm. She was trembling, but I did not know if it was from fear or anger. I steered her into a big waiting-room, out the door into the snow, through the snow to a clump of officials at the foot of the portable stairs leading to the cabin of the Comet Jet airliner. Here I handed over a couple of boarding passes. With that my passport and Tamara's were thrust into my hands.

"My God," I said to Tamara, "I'd forgotten all about the passports."

Ahead of me, she fairly skipped up the steps. She walked up the aisle and took a seat as far from the doorway as she could go. I sat down beside her, and took her hand.

"Everything's all right," I said. "It's all over. Relax."

"It won't be over until we reach the—" A Soviet official of some sort emerged from the airliner's cabin. For a moment I thought he was going to stop at our seat, but he moved on. Turning my head slightly, I saw him leave the plane.

"What were you saying?"

"It won't be over until we get across the Soviet frontier," she said.

"Well, that'll be in just a few minutes."

Actually, we did not leave for another hour and forty-two minutes. The crew had trouble warming up one of the engines. Several cryptic announcements in English over the plane's loudspeaker system made it plain that the Russian ground crew had not kept the engines as warm as they should have.

At last, however, we slowly rumbled out for the take-off, and then at the end of the runway we seemed to wait an eternity before we finally charged northward into what seemed the very teeth of a blizzard.

"God of mine," shuddered Tamara, "if we do get off the ground we'll all get killed."

"Nonsense," said I.

Airborne at last, there came that moment when a member of the crew comes out of the pilot's control center and walks down the aisle. I stopped the officer and said as unemotionally as I could, "We would greatly appreciate it if you would let us know when we have crossed over the Soviet frontier."

"I heard about your trouble with the customs and security," said the officer. "They can be bloody sometimes."

In a more confidential tone, he added, "I hope you didn't mind the early plane call. It would have been more comfortable if we had let you wait in the waiting-room, but we felt if we announced the plane was about to leave, well, that seemed the best way to break up the row."

"You were very perceptive," I told him.

"Oh," he laughed, "your wife wasn't the first to have departure trouble."

"Don't forget about the frontier, please."

"It'll be a pleasure."

For the second time on this trip I truly sweated out the time. Then came the announcement I had been straining to hear:

"Ladies and gentlemen, we have now crossed over the Soviet frontier."

Tamara squeezed my hand very tightly—and let out a long sigh.

"Hoaney," she said, "we're going home. Could I have a drink?"

I ordered champagne, and we settled back in our seats. "Darling," I asked, "do you know why I like champagne so much?"

"No, why, hoaney?"

"Because it's like you, it's so Russian. I even like the way you Russians say it, *champansky*."